CONTENTS

I0020998

AKRAM AHMAD

Dispatches from the Software Trenches:
Essays at the Intersection of Ideas, Programming, and Culture

Copyright © 2021 by Akram Ahmad.

All rights reserved.

FOREWORD

Let's Start Here...

This whole thing started with a blog I created earlier this century, right around 2014. Being a fellow creative type—we software types do get a kick out of doing what we do for a living, don't we?—I was looking for a creative outlet at that time, a channel if you will, for my creative doings (my undoing?)

Well, rather than bore you with how one thing led to another, and stuff like "Which school I went to, what I majored in, etc."—you can, should you wish, find all that at these coordinates—let's get on with the fun stuff, shall we?

Trivia fact: My name has an honorary mention in a book published last year by The MIT Press.

So yeah, as we sail right past the obligatory stuff (the one which leavens—or *leadens*, depending your perspective —other people's ocean-sized forewords), allow me to boil the ocean with these sentiments: I'm hard-core technical; I'm also hard-core into writing.

Or, as I was chatting with a friend just the other day:

> *The two things which nobody will ever wrest out of my DNA are (1) my writerly self, and (2) my programmer self.*

(Not necessarily in that order, though, I should've added.)

Oh, *this* you need to know: If I haven't bored you to tears already—though I sure hope I haven't!—please know that my writing style resonates with and is utterly permeated by the sentiment of the following, pithy saying:

> *My method is to take the utmost trouble to find the right thing to say, and then to say it with the utmost levity.*
> *- George Bernard Shaw*

And I'm *definitely* going to spare you the wherewithal of why—and also, *when* and *where*—my muse dubbed me a sprezzatura...

And now...

Something About You

I imagine that you are the sort of person who enjoys reading—books, magazines, blog posts, that kind of stuff—and doesn't equate this noble pastime with, say, a visit to the dentist for root canal.

I also imagine that your reading interests veer in the direction of the creative and the technical.

The way I see it, most of us who make a living in the tech industry—hence the name of this book, Dispatches from the Software Trenches—were attracted to the field in the first place by the near-infinite possibilities it offers us (to stretch our creative and technical muscles.)

If that describes you, even remotely so, dare I say you're in for a treat. Read on to find why I make so bold a claim.

What You can Expect

I have, in a decidedly pseudorandom way, gone through my blog posts—I prefer calling them essays, though this latter term has somehow fallen out of favor in our diaspora—from the past six years and selected the ones that resonated with me. (Kind of like the hits, to my mind anyway!)

Judging by the volume of readership—about 120,000 at my original blog and about 40,000 and-counting-and-losing-track at my current blog site, one to which I had migrated right around end-of-2018—the blog has done well. Really well.

My eternal gratitude to each and every one who has made the time to check the musings, and for coming back, over and over.

And why is that? Why have readers rewarded me over and over? (Heh, I'm not questioning you. Goodness, no. Just thinking aloud...)

My best guess is that readers enjoy stuff—the stuff of essays, to be precise—which is at the cusp of ideas, programming, and culture.

Brief Table of Contents

Here, then, is the proverbial 50,000 feet view of what awaits you in the pages that follow:

And with that, we're ready to set sail on the journey...

Bon Voyage!

Here's the deal: Every time I come across a new book, I find myself feverishly jumping to its foreword: Next thing you know—as I read the author spill his (or her) guts—I can't help but wonder how the lucky stiff got his (or her) work published!

And here I am, writing a foreword to my very own book, a book written just for you, of course, the better to help you get your bearings.

I hop that these thoughts will set you on the journey that lies ahead, waiting in the wings of these pages.

Be a part of the journey. Let me know what your reactions are. (I share my coordinates in just a bit.)

◆ ◆ ◆

MY COORDINATES

Should you wish to contact me—and I invite contact—any and *all* of the following work:

Blog: Programming Digressions: Essays

LinkedIn: This is a good way to stay in touch with me

Twitter: I occasionally *do* tweet

Github: My open source contributions page

◆ ◆ ◆

TESTIMONIALS

I nearly left this section out—we geeks tend to shy away from talking about ourselves, don't we?

So yeah, the only reason I did decide to retain this section is to level-set, because chances are that you haven't heard of me: Sort of to help you get to know me a bit better (and where my ideas and I come from. "Go to the source," as the adage would have it, amirite?)

With that, here are some blurbs—and here I headed over to my LinkedIn profile to grab a handful of testimonials—ones that you just might find interesting. (Should you start to tire, please feel free to sail right past this stuff, and jump into the book proper!)

One more time, we're just breaking the ice at this point...

Edward Lee
Robert S. Pepper Distinguished Professor, EECS Department, UC Berkeley
June 22, 2018, Edward was Akram's mentor

Akram is a true artist who deftly practices the art and craft of writing. He has a deep insight into software technologies and writes about them with humor, poetry, and well-chosen illustrations. His blog is a delight to read. I recommend him highly!

Nicole Reineke
Distinguished Engineer at Dell Technologies
September 17, 2020, Akram worked with Nicole in the same group

You can always count on Akram for a thoughtful, insightful conversation and to push the boundaries of an idea. In our discussions with the MIT Media Lab, he was able to identify meaningful new applications for forward looking research. Akram is an exceptional communicator, able to clearly express thought leadership in a meaningful way. A pleasure to work with. See less

Balaji Varadarajan
Lead Software Engineer at CCC Information Services
July 6, 2017, Akram was senior to Balaji but didn't manage directly

Its my honor and privilege to write a recommendation for Akram who is one of the finest human-being I have ever worked with. I still remember my first month at CCC & it was the same time when Akram was tied up with multiple high-priority tasks. Inspite of his busy schedule, not once he shied away from answering my questions and always motivated me to be curious. Akram always goes above & beyond when it comes to helping his peers & technically adept at tackling any challenging task put-forth. As a true believer of Steve Jobs' famous quote - "Stay hungry.. Stay foolish", Akram never misses an opportunity to learn new things & humility is one of his biggest strengths. I wish him all the very best & again a true honor having him as my mentor. See less

kitty fassett
retired pianist
December 9, 2017, kitty and Akram were students together

As a brilliant translator and supremely gifted writer, Akram Ahmad draws inspiration from a prodigious knowledge of a world of great literature and poetry. His blogs, decorated always with the perfect choice of artwork, flow with charm and originality and are a feast for the eyes and a joy to read.

Jim White
Chief Technology Officer at IOTech Systems
July 22, 2016, Jim was Akram's teacher

Akram was a former student of mine and now he is often my technology guide. Along with being a genuine, caring and nice person, Akram is now my technical debt meter. I have lunch with Akram every month or so. He is an incredible study of our industry and often understands where it is heading and why it's going there. After every lunch, I come away with lots of homework for myself on technologies I need to research and books I need to read (and often he is supplying the latter). He is a skilled engineer and deep thinker. Every organization could use about a dozen Akrams - we'd all be better for it. See less

Eric Bruno
Senior Principal Engineering Technologist - Edge and IoT Research
October 23, 2020, Akram worked with Eric in the same group

Very few people possess the passion, energy, and shear excitement for technology that Akram does. The dual drive he has for both the technology and the will to be successful is above what I've seen in almost everyone I've worked with. From coding, to machine learning, to deployment and customer engagement, and mundane tasks such as documentation, Akram puts all of himself into every bit of it. His positivity is inspiring and his drive to go above and beyond is unparalleled. From his day-to-day tasks and beyond, Akram strives to be a leader, including starting and driving the book club within our organization and doing awe inspiring research and sharing the results willingly with everyone. Underlying all of this is his unending drive and enjoyment in learning, helping others to learn and grow, and being equally inspired from what he can learn from others. It's this sort of collaboration that turns good ideas into great ones, and helps organizations grow from being a development group to a truly innovative powerhouse. Give him the opportunity to show you what true leadership and innovation is, and you won't be let down. See less

Okay, that'll do for now. (In all seriousness, though, I am oh-so humbled by these—and other—testimonials I've received over the years. I truly am, straight up from the heart!)
And hey, so nice to meet you, dear Reader—Welcome to the book you hold in your hands!

With that, the very first chapter coming right up...

◆ ◆ ◆

CHAPTER 1: THE 5 MOST VALUABLE LESSONS FOR PROGRAMMERS

A dreamer is one who can only find his way by moonlight, and his punishment is that he sees the dawn before the rest of the world.
- Oscar Wilde

0. Boiling The Ocean

If I had to distill what I've learned in my programming career that spans over two decades now—and going strong—it would boil down to the following five lessons:

1. Diversify
2. Read
3. Write
4. Seek Mentors And Mentor Others
5. Find Your Passion

"Why five? Why not 10 or 15 or more?", you might well ask... Fair questions both.

First, in asking me to share *more* than five lessons—trust me, I've got plenty more that I could share—you run the risk of opening Pandora's Box because of my well-known propensity (notoriety, in the mind of some) for exploring ever-widening swathes of related ideas.

Second, this is the age of the soundbite, one to which I could have remained immune for only so long... (Trust me, I can write plenty more, secure in the knowledge that many of you will enjoy it, but acutely aware at the same time that some of you might find your eyes glazing over at my whale-like paragraphs.)

Third, a happy medium of five lessons suggested itself to me; not too little, not too much. So that's what you get this time around (Should you wish for more, simply ping me and I'll be happy to share more!)

With that, let's dive right in to the top five lessons that came to my mind unbidden, almost subliminally. See, this is what happens—subliminal stuff and somnambulism and scorching metaphors and whatnot—when one starts quoting Edgar Allen

Poe and his squawking raven as I have in recent essays!

1. My Use Of The Term "Programmer"

It seems pretty reasonable to say that the image which the term "programmer" will conjure up in your mind is one of "software designers", "software engineers", "computer scientists", and such.

This group of practitioners—of which I happen to be one—lies on a spectrum so I feel comfortable in generalizing (the term "programmer") to the even *broader* spectrum of technologists and, frankly, all practitioners who are looking to raise the level of their game.

Yes, the diving board above is there for a purpose now: to launch you into the deep blue waters of the inviting swimming pool above for some free—yes, free as in air—les-

sons on the practice of programming.

Ready to dive right in? (Our craft is vast, and our lifetime *all* too brief)

So let's go into the uncharted universe, starting with those oh-so fabulous rings around the planet Saturn.

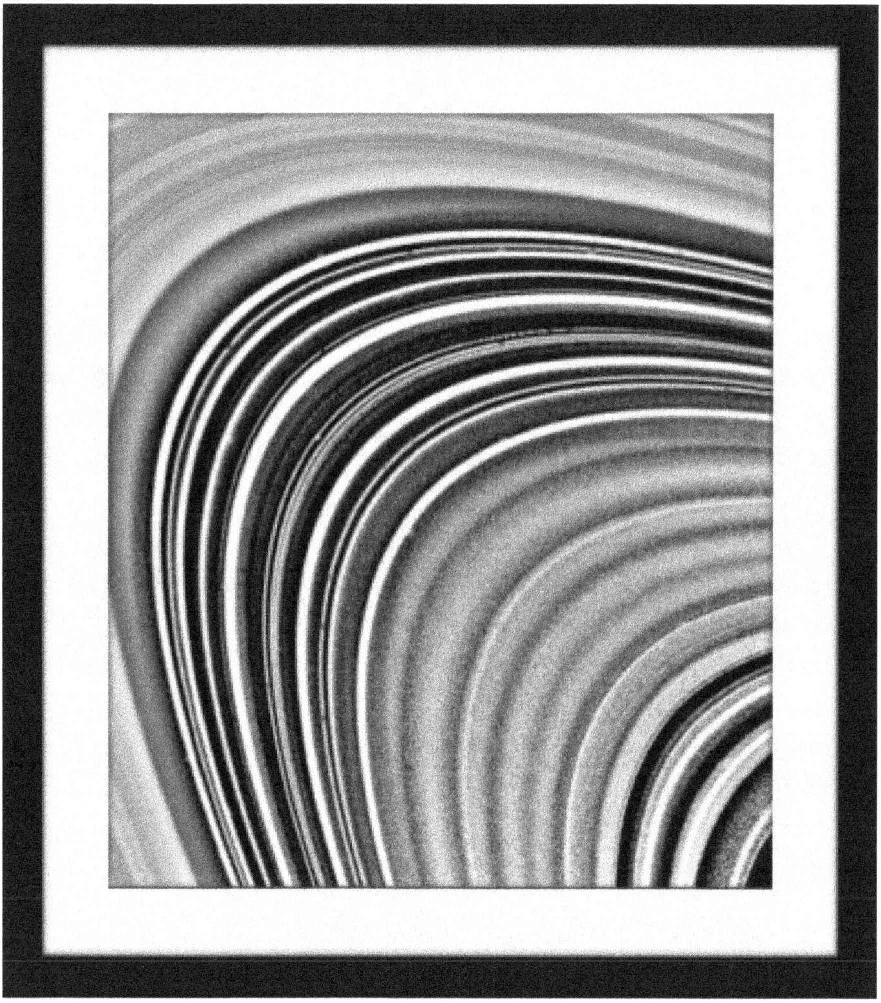

2. Lesson #1: Diversify

See the Saturn rings in the picture above? And no, we are not entering the twilight zone of diversifying financial portfolios and bean-counting either—stuff best left to financial wizards.

We *are*, however, very much diving head-first into the ocean that is the realm of a (sustainable) career in the world of programming. More specifically, think of this dive as an exploration of the wellsprings that can fuel your passion over the long haul.

First, though, let me tell you about the wellspring of my inspiration for choosing "Diversify" as the very first lesson that I want to share with you... It goes back to an article in a programming magazine by one of my programming heroes, the late John Vlissides.

Way back then, when I was designing programs in the C++ programming language, I read an article by Vlissides that was intriguingly titled "*Forget C++!*" I did a double take, as you can imagine, before settling down to devour the new nuggets of wisdom which Vlissides was about to share...

In a nutshell, his message was this: Diversify—never allow the narrowing of your vision. And to which I would like to add that the narrowing of one's vision is right up there with the clogging of one's arteries. You'll want to avoid *both*!

> *Hmm... Something having to do with "reading" coming up, amirite?*

READ

3. Lesson #2: Read

As they say, a nation of readers is a nation of leaders. Closer at hand—as I've come to understand how this advice applies to the world of programming—read programs written by great programmers, programmers whose work you admire. All great writers were readers once. And while the reading process, once begun, should never really end, it simply has to begin. It is through exposure to great programs that (and this is where the lesson to read comes in) you learn how to write great programs.

I can trace this priceless listen to a piece of advice from *The Pragmatic Programmers*: the duo of Dave Thomas and Andy Hunt...

In the end, and even if you forget everything else, please remember this: Taking a leaf from the gardeners and farmers of the world, let us—*after* of course taking a cue from my nemesis the Bard to get rid of all the language lawyers—go out in earnest and Read The Farming Manual (I mean, our brethren the UNIX gurus have exactly the right sort of idea in admonishing us all to *RTFM*)

Behold those instruments of writing now coming into sight... Those quills and papyrus scrolls just might be a sign of things to come.

4. Lesson #3: Write

Lest you jump to the conclusion that the tools in the picture above are what I use for writing, I should hasten to add that—much as I wish they were—they are not. Alas, and this is a long story, we stopped writing (I imagine this applies to the vast majority of fellow humans on planet Earth) in longhand. Sigh...

But all is not lost; we have at our disposal a reasonably good set of alternate tools to ply the craft of writing (both prose *and* programs). Yay!

"No impression without expression", so goes an intriguing adage that I came across in the pages—gulp, I do confess to having been a fan boy, decades ago—of the once-venerable Readers Digest magazine. So what does this have to do with *programming*? Nothing, and everything! Let me explain...

Tying this lesson back to the previous one—the advice to "Read"—while reading is a great start, it is just that: a start. To get anywhere, you simply *have* to take the next step, which is to write your own programs and thereby hone your proficiency at writing programs (Should you ever start forgetting, remind yourself that programming is not a spectator sport!). Other things remaining the same, the more you write, the better you get (within reasonable limits such as taking crucial aspects of, for example, feedback and quality.)

Moving right on: If you are anything like me, ready to take on the software complexity monster, a mentor or two is what I'd like by my side...

5. Lesson #4: Seek Mentors, And Mentor Others

See the warrior in the image above, fearlessly standing his ground even as he wields his weapons to slay the complexity monster? He is doing it alone. However, much as there is a rightful place for heroics, it doesn't have to be that way—there are saner approaches to taming the green-eyed monster that is the sprawling expanse of software writ large...

Everyone was a beginner once, on their way to becoming a journeyman, and then an expert. And this is where mentoring comes in: seek mentors, and once you become an expert yourself, please make sure to keep the virtuous cycle going by mentoring others!

> *Shall we check some time-lapse photography, and what symbolism lies in wait for us? I say we check what permeating the ethos of this beguiling picture...*

6. Lesson #5: Find Your Passion

As you take in the time-lapse photography in the lovely picture above, I want you to keep in mind the overarching, all-encompassing slant that I hope you will see permeating the ethos of the picture...

If I had to boil down all the lessons I've learned in the practice of programming—distill everything down to an uber lesson—this would be it: Go and find your passion...

And I'm not talking about some fairy-tale romance or arabesque musings. No, nothing of that sort; well, *mostly* nothing of that sort. After all, passion and prose *do* have to connect somewhere, they do have to intertwine something...

But what I have in mind, and what I want to share here—without this particular lesson turning into a whole new essay of its own—is far more workmanlike (*and* work-woman-like, to be sure!) It is simply this: motivation is hugely important, so take up this business of finding your passion in great earnest! Let me share a pointer or two in this connection:

- A Retrospective of The year 2017
- Finding Your Spark

Good enough for now?

Use your health, even to the point of wearing it out. That is what it is for. Spend all you have before you die; do not outlive yourself.
- George Bernard Shaw

In ending this chapter, I seek to honor the overarching (undercurrents of the) theme of the oneness of humanity which I've done my best to honor in this essay, and the imprints of which you may well have discerned in the images I've carefully chosen.

Let's bring this essay to a close, reaffirm that the most important lesson of all is to keep our faith in the oneness of humanity as the basis for what is the very best of spending the fleetingly little time we've been given on the wondrous planet that we call Earth...

◆ ◆ ◆

CHAPTER 2: WHAT I SAW AT GOPHERCON 2019

Check the marquee, and the hallway abuzz with activity!

0. Welcome to the Show, Gophers!

Imagine seeing the world through the eyes of a gopher (I'm talking about the furry rodent, by the way). On top of that, just to make things fun, now imagine transporting our gopher somehow to the beach-side city that is San Diego, where a bunch—and I mean hordes—of Go programmers (aka Gophers) are about to converge for an annual pilgrimage.

Yep, the annual GopherCon event is about as big as it gets for us Gophers.

What you get from all that, as you may well have guessed by now, is one giddy gopher!

And I'm here to tell you a story that has never been told before, at least not quite like this: Summoning all the powers of empathy at my disposal, I have—in the fine tradition of the fanciful flight that is the metaphorical fugue enshrined in the pages of Douglas Hofstadter's Pulitzer Prize-winning book *Gödel, Escher, Bach: An Eternal Golden Braid*—braided together the furry rodent's world-view with mine (last time I checked, I was still a non-furry human being).

Hey, I say, that's plenty good for setting the stage. It's nearly showtime. So we're going to call our intros good, and join a behind-the-scenes tour of the amazing show that has been GopherCon 2019 in San Diego.

(Oh, and never mind the levitating rodent in the picture above of the conference hotel lobby, the one wearing what looks like *The Sorting Hat* from the *Harry Potter* movies—I'm quite sure the rodent wasn't a part of the welcoming committee, and merely under the spell of a good old *Wingardium Leviosa* magical incantation. And yes, I know my gophers from my rats from my lemmings from...

Yeah, more on lemmings later; quite a bit more.

1. First Impressions

One thing that really, really stood out for me is just how friendly and welcoming the worldwide community of Go programmers truly is—it's a fond memory I've brought back home with me to Austin. Yours truly (remember that I get to play the role of a non-furry human being in this tale) found gophers of all stripes to be eminently accessible.

Just to take one example, and if you would be so kind as to crane your neck upwards a bit to take in the picture above, I'm standing on the GopherCon 2019 floor (in San Diego) with the Go programming language tech lead at Google, Russ Cox, a really smart and down-to-earth guy. Many of you already know both—or at least one—of us, but should you need to disambiguate who is who, I gently direct you to check the conference badge each hanging from our respective neck.

Gotta tell ya, it's awesome to come into contact with fellow Gophers who make up our vibrant and friendly community. We all contribute, in ways big and small. In my own (small) way, I've been contributing for a while now to an open source project that is powered primarily by the Go programming language—polyglot though that project remains since its inception—and which is hosted by the Linux Foundation: EdgeX Foundry.

Open source projects are cool. I urge you to join one today!

SPLASH!
SEAPORT VILLAGE

2. So Is This Where Lemmings Jump Off?

For the faint of heart—lest you break into a frenzy of panic—I hasten to add that the meme of lemmings jumping en masse (off the edge of the cliff) has been debunked. Yet it remains a prevalent and persistent myth. Go figure.

Oh, and never you mind the splash "sound" in the picture above. It was just me, sprucing up a picture I took on the very first morning after checking into my room at the hotel at the Marina in San Diego, the venue of GopherCon 2019.

Seaport Village—check the tasteful banner above—is an endearing spot for tourists of all stripes, gophers very much included (More soon on a related adventure that took place a scant 100 yards away, on the esplanade down from the sailboats-bedecked harbor. So stay tuned.)

Hey, speaking of traversing the physical landscape—and I invite you to think of this essay as a travelogue of sorts—two other fairly recent travelogues come to mind, the following, the first one of which was to a tech conference that took place in Edinburgh, Scotland, and the second one in Seoul, South Korea:

1. *Yer Edinburgh Ode to Microservices*
2. The Soul of Edge Computing

Disclaimer: Please don't expect *National Geographic*-level material; just to remind you, I'm (only) a veteran software engineer and architect, nowhere near the inimitable naturalist David Attenborough!

WOW!

3. Thou Shalt Register

So I did.

Hey, for all the naysayers out there—and I know there's a few of you out there right now—check the picture above where your friendly gopher (the non-furry kind) can be spotted, having dutifully worked his way through lines of fellow gophers, emerging with my trophies: conference badge, the canonical T-shirt, and all.

So there you have it, my *Good Housekeeping* proof-of-purchase!

And for those of you who haven't run away yet in disbelief—remember, I warned you at the outset that this tale aims to remain faithful to the fanciful flight of a metaphorical fugue in the evergreen tradition of Hofstadter's *Gödel, Escher, Bach: An Eternal Golden Braid*—I give you a pat on the back.

Welcome again. The show is about to begin...

GOPHERCON
GOPHERCON
00:00

4. Woohoo, Speaker Highlights

In full candor, I was oh-so pleased by the high quality of the talks. I sure learned a ton of Go programming tactics, techniques, and strategies to bring back and apply to my own work.

For the past one year—and this is to establish some context so we're on the same page—yours truly, an industry veteran in the area of architecting and implementing distributed computing software systems, and used to extensively wielding tools from the Java and Scala ecosystems, has been swimming full-time in the ocean that has arisen from the amazing language that is Go.

Relax, I'm not about to go meta; to drive the marine metaphors home, though, let's just say that the beaches of San Diego were an especially appropriate venue for hosting the conference.

Back to the GopherCon 2019 talks now. These are the ones that stand out, and here I present merely a snapshot impression each. So in no particular order, other than this being the order in which I recall them, they were by the following speakers:

Elena Morozova

I appreciated a lot how Elena's talk (*How Uber "Go"es*) was delightfully replete with helpful, thoughtful, and often times humorous illustrations which shone a new light on an indispensable subject: How does one go about maintaining a large codebase for maximum readability and minimal overhead? In addition to being really well done, the talk was candid. Elena shared the challenges Uber faced in that process—including places where they ran into the occasional failure or two—yet emerged with successful solutions. Referring back to my notes, I remember now that Elena had also talked about actually introducing a software tool to actually *enforce* consistent code structure ("Glue" was that project name, and I'll definitely be visiting that soon). All in all, excellent talk. Neat stuff.

◆ ◆ ◆

Marwan Sulaiman

The terrific thing about Marwan's talk (*Handling Go Errors*) was the incredibly deftness with which he walked us through an actual use case of going about solving a complex problem by *thinking* in the unique paradigms of Go (Anyone remember the excellent *Thinking in Java* book from way back when? Hint: I want its counterpart for Go!) Anyhow, I can attest to the wisdom of resisting the urge to go your own way; instead, the way to go is to lean on the philosophy with which Go has been designed to solve programming problems. And hey, even if error-handling is not your heartthrob topic—I honestly can't claim it has ever been mine—the way Marwan brought programmable errors to life (in how you can design your own architecture in this area, enabling you to get a solid grip on system failures) was cool. I was wowed. Frankly, an outstanding talk.

◆ ◆ ◆

Mat Ryer

If I were asked to point to (only) one talk which did an outstanding job of stripping away all *accidental* complexity, leading me and others in the audience to keep a laser sharp focus instead on the *essential* complexity of problem-solving in the domain at hand—adhering to the elegance of the Go way of doing things—it would be Mat's talk (*How I Write HTTP Web Services After Eight Years*). So I've done this sort of thing at least 17 different ways in the past—using assorted tools from libraries that have evolved around more mature languages such as Java and Scala—Mat demonstrated just how elegantly (and simply!) it all can be done with Go. A talk (whose recording now) is not to be missed.

◆ ◆ ◆

Katie Hockman

What made Katie's talk (*Go Module Proxy: Life of a Query*) so compelling was the command with which she had masterfully assembled a whole boatload of hardcore tech subtopics into a unified whole and the conviction with which she presented her stuff. Trust me, delving into the intricacies of how her team built a module mirror and checksum database is not for the faint of heart. But Katie somehow managed to pull it off, never for a moment shying from the guts of what makes authenticated module proxies tick (Merkle Trees and all!) The delightfully humorous (running) backdrop of "the dog people" versus "the cat people" was well done and genuinely engaging. And hey, from now on I will remember her advice to "Trust on *your* first use"! (At least that's what my scribbled notes say; more on that later.)

◆ ◆ ◆

Russ Cox

I was expecting nothing less than exceptional quality from the talk (*On the Road to Go 2*) by Russ and came away really pleased. Let me remind you that this list of speakers that I've assembled here is in no particular order, other than this being the order in which I recall some of the stellar talks. For those not familiar with his name—is there anyone, really?—Russ leads the development of the Go programming language. His talk was methodical, precise, and enlightening. I got a really good feel for how the Go language (itself) is being shepherded and evolved (Simplify by reshaping, by redefining, etc. Abandoning failed experiments, growing stronger from the learnings. Etc.). Given that we're on the road to Go 2, the talk answered the questions of(1) Where exactly are we? and (2) Where are we headed? I sure am glad I came to the fantastic talk by Russ to get the answers to exactly those burning questions.

◆ ◆ ◆

Ian Lance Taylor

The subject of Ian's talk (*Generics in Go*) is incredibly dear to me, making it virtually a guaranteed success even before I heard a word of his splendid talk. I was pleased. Very pleased. Coming from a heavy background in Java and Scala—where generics rule the day—I've been hankering for generics since the day I immersed myself in Go programming over a year ago. Fast-forward one year to today, and Ian's team continues to work hard to make genetics a reality for us gophers. He rightly pointed out that when it happens (i.e. when generics become a part of Go), programming should feel no different—become no more esoteric—than when working with the usual constructs: Yep, while there are clear advantages to introducing generics into Go, there also happen to be associated a bunch of requirements. Keep up the good work, Ian and team.

Oh, and FWIW, I took copious notes. I felt *compelled* to; yes, to be sure, the awesome conference organizers do make the slide decks available, yet this inveterate note-taking engineer continues to find that the best way to internalize complex subject matter is by way of pen and paper. (Physical) action does shape thought, methinks. (Hey, if it isn't you again, in your naysayer splendor, kind of! Looks like you want to see for yourself my *Good Housekeeping* seal-of-approval of sorts... Let me tell you, I'll prove myself trustworthy. Should you *still* need to see my seal-of-approval, I've got that, too. You stay tuned.)

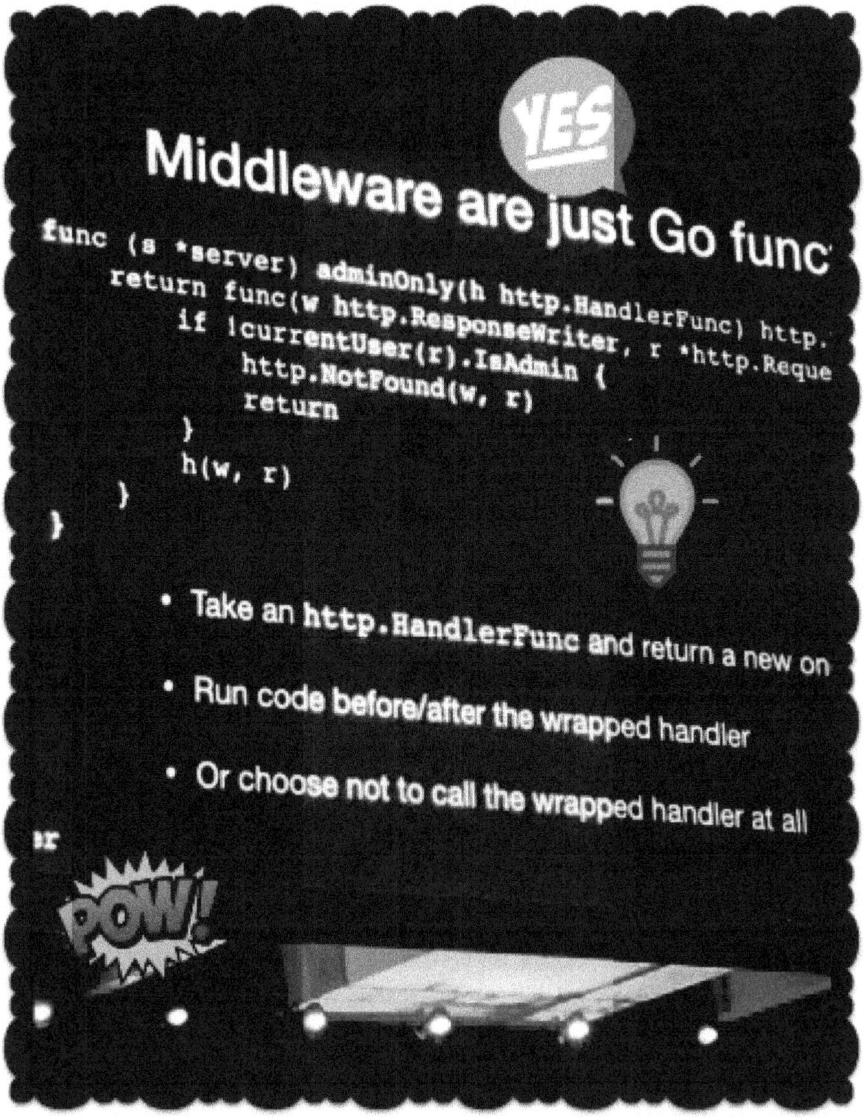

5. There Is No Middleware

Oh wait, that bold statement was from, or at least inspired by, a line from The Matrix ("There is no spoon"), now wasn't it? Darn. Never mind. Scratch that one.

There is—and probably will be for the rest of our living days —*plenty* of middleware in the wild for us gophers to rummage through. And if you want to work with it without pulling your hair out, may I suggest that you listen to what Mat Ryer has to say on the subject? I took the picture above—all pictures that appear in this essay were taken by yours truly, on site, in the spirit of "*Kilroy was here*"!—in an inspired moment during Mat's talk (*How I Write HTTP Web Services After Eight Years*).

And hey, hats off to the conference organizers—the names of Erik St. Martin and Brian Ketelsen jump to mind as I was already familiar with seeing their names from their *Forewords* to Go programming books—for making sure that there were a bunch of strategically-placed overhead (and, *thankfully*, oversized!) monitors in the ballrooms where the numerous talks were presented.

The picture above shows one such monitor in action; the thingamajigs and sound effects, as you have likely guessed by now, are mine alone (Yo, I snuck those embellishments in when nobody was looking. Truth be told, this blogs comes to you from a one-man-shop, so the number of people watching would've been approximately zero, zilch, nada).

One more time, for good measure—and please repeat after me this time—this *narrative* (sheesh, did I really call it a *tale* earlier?) aims to remain faithful to the fanciful flight of imagination in the evergreen tradition of *Gödel, Escher, Bach: An Eternal Golden Braid*. Hence the embellishments, amirite?

6. Gophers, Too, Get Hungry

Just sayin'. Our stomachs, too, rumble at times. Seriously, though, we were kept well-fed with sumptuous, catered meals. What redoubled our joy of dining, though, was chatting with a bunch of fellow gophers at the plethora of circular dining tables that decked the Pacific ballroom.

We had a bunch of active and energizing discussions about how we gophers are going about attacking problems with the Go tools at our disposals.

By the way, and just by the way, see if you can spot an especially oversized—mutant, dare I say?—burger over there yonder, starboard, mostly to the left of my right shoulder... Folks, stand back: That one's mine!

Oh, and taking a page from a talk by Mat Ryer—right here at GopherCon 2019 in San Diego—I remind you of the obvious in that we all get *intellectually* hungry, too. We happen to have the mindset of insatiable curiosity, always eager to learn better ways of solve programming problems, designing more robust solutions, and stuff like that. So go ahead and touch someone's life for the better by sharing your experience through blogging.

Well, when it comes to blogging on Go, here's a sampling of stuff I've written up over the past one year or so:

- *Best Go Programming Books (2019)*
- *The Go Programming Language*
- *Further Adventures In Go Land*

Oh, and speaking of the art of *writing* itself... (Wait, what's that murmuring I hear!) Ah, but of course: I can almost sense (some of) my regular readers groaning—who know full well my fondness for digressing—and are now beckoning me to spare *you* the agony. But you know what? Practicing the art of writing is supremely enjoyable. So here you go, geek-out on a take on the craft by one person, yours truly. Woohoo!:

- *On Writing: Or Why I Write*
- *On Writing: Or How I Write*
- *On Writing: Or Wow I Write*
- *On Writing: Or Now I Write*
- *On Writing: Or A Row With How I Write*

While you read those musings, I'm going to wait for you right here...

Ah, you're back. Good. Let's see, if that doesn't convince you that anyone—virtually *anyone*—can write, please take two pills and call your doctor in the morning (for a full cranial-checkup referral). Thanks.

7. We Do ML & AI With Go!

On returning home to Austin, I had made a promise to myself to do a write up on the learnings that I've taken away from the awesome, daylong workshop (on ML/AI using Go) to share with you. Little did I know at that time my starry-eyed idea would transform into a full-fledged essay, one you're reading; you still with me?

Pat yourself on the back if you've made it this far.

Anyhow, and while I know a thing or two about AI—my MS thesis back in the day involved designing and creating a hefty chunk of neural networks code, of the back-propagation algorithm species, if that means anything to anyone, in the C programming language—it is only recently that I've begun to see why Go (with its awesome heft in the concurrency area especially) is positioned so nicely to carve a niche for itself in the area of ML/AI.

Oh, the places a programming language will take you when something so crucial (to making hay in today's multicore world) as concurrency is baked right into the language!

And never mind all those levitating objects with which I've embellished *yet* another picture I took outside the entrance of our packed classroom.

JOIN US NEXT TIME...
WOW!
COOL

8. Inside The Wizards' Room

Our excellent instructor, Daniel Whitenack, was ably assisted by his fellow data scientist, Miriah Peterson. In addition to all the hands-on coding we gophers eagerly did—with our furry paws, of course—we got to see a ton of cool demonstrations.

For example, you'll see above how Daniel is putting all the clout of ML & AI Go libraries into identifying that most essential of all objects that populate a programmer's universe: the coffee cup.

So we did neural networks in Go, followed by a helpful foray —using Go as our implementation mechanism, of course— through the area of Deep Learning. Speaking of which, I would be remiss if I didn't share the coordinates of some stuff I've written up on that very subject:

1. *Best Deep Learning Books (Pragmatic)*
2. *Best Deep Learning Books (Foundational)*
3. *Best Deep Learning Books (Popular)*

Plenty for now? Okay, okay, if you want me to *also* throw some AI in there—and we might as well get our paws on it—here's some (hopefully) helpful stuff by yours truly that you can check out, too:

1. *Why I Worry About AI (Artificial Intelligence)*
2. *Supercharge Your Understanding Of Superintelligence!*

Cool?

JUST AT THAT MOMENT...
BOING!
Free daily 30 minute JUMP rides

9. Go Code Even Powers Bike Logistics

To the denizens of the stellar rodent family we've encountered so far—gophers, rats, and lemmings—let's add the good old bunny, shall we? It's only fair to do so, I think, given the central position our bunny has assumed in the picture above.

Speaking of which, I noticed this when I ventured outside the conference hotel one fine day: Our good friends at Uber are powering transportation logistics with software written (most likely, though I would need to confirm) in Go!

So there you go.

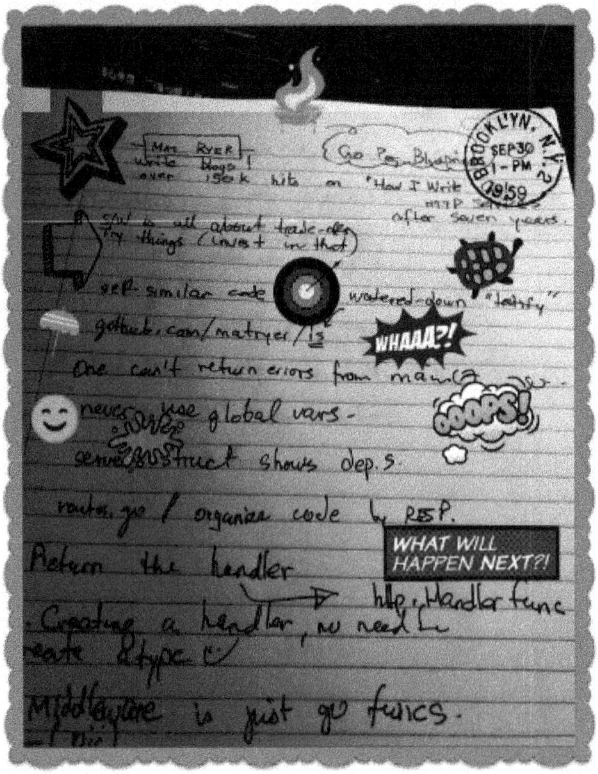

10. I Took Notes (Lots Of Them!)

Well, I have space here to show but a page or two, all in my longhand writing, which was—as you can likely tell by the shaky, calligraphic penmanship sample above—all done at warp speed as yours truly did his best to keep up with the swift pace of all the fine speakers who spoke at the stage (Anyone tried drinking water from the proverbial fire-hose?)

This particular page—the one above with my pseudo-calligraphic penmanship on display—comes from a talk by one of my favorite technical writers, the excellent Mat Ryer, author of a terrific book named *Go Programming Blueprints*.

Keep up the cool work, Mat. You're an inspiration to this gopher!

11. When Nighttime Falls

Sleep may be overrated, but gophers, too, need to sleep. We're not nocturnal, you know. Just sayin'. But hey, what did I see one night when peering from my hotel room's magnificent balcony—all the way up on the 19th floor—at the Marina landscape outside? Oh my!

It's on you now—See if you can spot the following themes in the pic above:

- A raven (swooping in its stealthy flight)
- A mutant owl (cleverly perched along the Marina curb-side)
- Another renegade, mutant, actually a feline friend (smack in the middle of the Marina intersection!)
- Oh, Batman, too?

Okay, I'm outta here, folks.

LET'S
EAT!
JOIN US NEXT TIME...

12. Breakfast Is Served

Won't you join us next time? Please. Pretty please? Just so you know, we gophers are real gregarious.

I can't promise, though, that you, too, will be privy to spying a whale or two, blowing mist in one of the swimming pools yonder—your YMMV (In this gilded age of fake news, there's even more to be said for truth-in-advertising, isn't there?)

13. Your Lips Move, But…

…I can't hear what you say.

Darn. Did you, fine creatures that you all three patently are, really have to speak in empty (speech) bubbles! Like, do to you *really* want me to dig up my copy of Jurafsky and Martin's classic text *Speech and Language Processing* and get to work on designing and decoding what you cuties are trying to tell me? (Especially you there in the middle, Ms. Owl, what kind of designs do *you* have, rolling your eyes like that?)

14. I Inventoried (The Cover Of) My Mac's Lid...

...before and after GopherCon 2019, to get a ballpark metric on just how fecund—*or* barren—my stickers menagerie is. So the picture above being the "before" one.

I'm not quite sure how my personal business card of sorts made it into the picture (That's why I was trying to shine a flashlight, as you can tell). Anyhow, the rest of the story will be told later.

Don't you go away!

15. The GopherCon Floor

As you can probably tell from the selfie above—taken in complete sincerity for the sake of coverage—the floor was abuzz with active discussions during one of the numerous thoughtfully-spaced-out program breaks.

And oh yes, it was bound to happen: With all that intellectual firepower concentrated in one place, a brainstorm or two was bound to emerge.

Needless to say, the *ZAP* above is my best artistic attempt to capture one especially potent thunderbolt during one such program break.

Good enough for now?

16. We Dive Right Back Into More Awesomeness

Wow, it sure was a ton of fun, sitting shoulder-to-shoulder with industry peers, all of us eagerly taking in Go programming wisdom by the bucketful. The metaphor of drinking water from the proverbial fire hydrant holds water and comes to mind, too.

Wait a second now!

How did that spunky yet harmless-looking alien above—you know the one with the foot long ears protruding from the generous head screwed atop its dwarfish torso—make it into my picture? Folks, this is an alien-sighting, I'm telling you.

But let's not get ruffled up: We gophers are eminently receptive to all species, including the alien kind. And who knows, we may be on the threshold of discovering a brand-new member of the sterling rodent family, woohoo!

Someone call *National Geographic*. Quick.

AARGH!
WHAT WILL
HAPPEN NEXT?!

17. How Does One Stop A Rhino From Charging?

Easy. You just take away its VISA (credit) card.

But you see, the dilemma I faced the following morning—having slumbered and dreamed of Go programming Tao and having dutifully counted flocks of sheep the night before—was *far* more ominous.

There I was, as you can tell from the picture above of the esplanade on the Marina, unwittingly immersed in the imbroglio involving a renegade hippo looking me squarely in the eyes.

Gulp.

Yo, sheep—are you one among the flocks in my dreams last night that I had counted or did you get away?—you *sure* look prim and smug and all. Grrr... Can you, like, wipe that cherubic grin from your face? I'm facing the dilemma of my lifetime, frantically trying to bail out of the dire situation, and you're posing as the very picture of serenity. Sigh, this is no time for venting.

Look, if this were merely a rhinoceros, I could've easily stopped it in its tracks (by taking away its VISA card, of course). But this happens to be a behemoth hippo, for crying out loud. What to do now?

AARGH!

My amygdala kicks in full time (heavens be praised for our evolutionarily-sound genetic makeup!) as I, or at least my *subliminal* self—frankly, I couldn't care less which one of those two it was in that moment of life-and-death—realize exactly what to do: Elements of maladroitness notwithstanding, I scurry at warp speed to the ocean inlet on my right and dive headlong into the safe waters, feeling secure in the knowledge that hippos don't swim.

Woohoo, I'm safe now, swimming in safe waters! After all, the distaste of hippos for water is matched *only* by the one harbored by cats. Right? (Or am I not up to snuff on my *National Geographic* magazine-based worldview of animal habits?)

What?! *Now* you tell me.

AARGH!

I hope I live to tell the rest of my tale...

18. Your Blogger Comes To His Senses

And when I came to, slowly waking up from my reverie-like slumber, everything was calm. Eerily calm. A bit too much so, I thought. But my premonition was unfounded.

All is well, I *think*.

Yay! The rest of the story can now be told:

- **For starters:** Remember the "before" picture from the "before and after" blurb earlier about GopherCon 2019, to get a ballpark metric on just how fecund—*or* barren—the stickers menagerie on my Mac's lid is evolving into? Well, I'm happy to report that (as you'll glean from the latest picture above, the "after"), we have indeed evolved. *Quite* a bit, too. Wont' you say?
- **Some more:** Ah, their lips had seemed to move—if you will turn your attention now to the three fine creatures we had a skirmish with, the ones that spoke only in monumentally unhelpful empty speech bubbles—and how one of them, Ms. Owl to be precise, seemed to have designs of her own. Guess what? Ms. Owl somehow interloped—not *eloped*, mind you, merely interloped—along with my baggage (on my flight back home from San Diego) and I unwittingly lugged her, feathers and all. Rats, don't they do any screening anymore for live animals in transit? Sigh. That cutie (you'll spy her toward the bottom left in the pic above) is standing pretty much shoulder to shoulder with my very own gopher mascot. Ms. Owl is looking all dainty (and smitten!) But by whom? Surely not *me*... I mean,

I'm just a *gopher*, you know.

- **Wait, there's even more:** The levitating rodent we had seen in the conference hotel lobby, the one wearing what looked like *The Sorting Hat* from the *Harry Potter* movies, was evidently *also* able to manage interloping with my baggage. Sigh! Our screening processes (for live animals in transit) are in tatters. And yikes! The rat's brought his *Sorting Hat* with him... Who knows what he'll transform into, and I'm not taking any chances. Calling dog pound right now. Um, or maybe the exterminators. Or something. Help!

In the remote possibility that you're still with me—I mean, dear reader, we've already been through a lot—let's collectively soothe our nerves. This, too, shall pass.

I promise.

19. Gulp. The Swallows, Akram, The Swallows

Allow me now to cite the farmers' wisdom when they say that if you sight a swallow or two—like the slick one above that barely missed your blogger's cranium while he was taking a selfie out a Seaport Village shop—and especially when they swoop close to the ground, a storm is surely brewing (I can, FWIW and in full sincerity, vouch to the veracity of the farmers' predictive wisdom; I have evidence for the strong correlation, just no explanation!)

Hey, what, exactly, is that green, dragonfly-like thingamajig (hovering over my shoulder) doing here, hovering about in its gossamer flight? Just at that moment, though...

Help!

As if my harrowing escape from the jaws of the juggernaut on the Marina esplanade—does anyone even remember the ferocious hippo and my plaintive pleas?—hadn't been enough, I find myself in the crosshairs of a smitten creature: Ms. Owl has declared her unrequited love for me in no uncertain terms (That teaches me a lesson to be careful and double-check what I'm lugging with me in all future travels!)

But there she is, drenched in the songs of innocence. Yo, and *I'm* perspiring profusely, drenched in sweat. Darn. What to do?

Anyone?

Ah yes. My evolutionarily-sound amygdala kicks into high gear again as innocent images of kindergarten days swim before my eyes: Owls, I feverishly recall, happen to be the very symbol of smarts, for crying out loud. So yes, I will appeal to Ms. Owl's reason. I got this one nailed.

Tentative at first, our conversation proceeds like so:

— **Akram, that's me, your blogger:** *Why, hello there, Ms. Owl, how* *goes it for you?*

— **Ms. Owl, batting her eyes:** *Swell. And for you?*

— **Akram:** *Say, since you happen to find yourself in my study, shall we, um, study?*

— **Ms. Owl, demurely:** *If you say so.*

— **Akram:** *I do. Yep, do please get going with the following reading material—this should keep you busy for a while—starting with an appropriately-nocturnal meditation for your owlish outlook:*

- *Reveling In The Glory Of Software (On A Stormy Night!)*
- *Krazy About Kafka!*
- *Plato And The Nerd Strikes Back*
- *Blockchain Adventures!*
- *Microservices In Small Pieces*

— **Ms. Owl:** *Okay, if you say so, sugar plum.*

— **Akram:** *Sheesh...* [I'm careful here, of course, to mutter under my breath so as to spare her owlish sensibilities].

Help! Ms. Owl here is showing no signs of slowing down. In fact, she has just spied my tome with the rather prosaic title of *HTTP: The Definitive Guide*, wedged as it was in one of the bookshelves in my library, and wants to regale me in the wisdom of the crucial role that HTTP plays in girding the very fabric of distributed computing, in particular the ins and outs of eventual consistency.

Man, I'm not getting anywhere. Somebody?

*Any*body!

SMACK!
THE END.

20. Afterword

Hey, we went right past The End. What's up with that?

Relax. Afterwards, one's gotta have an *Afterword*, or so I've been told...

So I didn't want to leave you hanging, wondering whatever became of the spring that had sprung in dainty Ms. Owl's heart...

This is what happened: Your trusty blogger—I've been called many things but you can call me Akram, yeah—had just about finished unpacking his suitcase on returning from San Diego (having bid farewell to hordes of friendly, fellow gophers) to his home in Austin when he felt something cushiony at the bottom of his suitcase.

Aha, there's my cutie gopher mascot—so I had purchased it at one of the Diversity Fund shops on the GopherCon floor—the mascot from which I was fearing I'd been separated! So I blithely placed my stuffed mascot atop the lowermost ledge of the jumbo bookshelf in my study upstairs. I even gave him a name: Mr. Jowl.

From the get go, I kinda' liked how it sounded (a gopher with such immaculately puffy cheeks ought to get a name befitting it!)

The rest, as they say, is history...

Remember Ms. Owl, the one scurrying about in my study, smitten twice-over, and lecturing me incessantly on the finer points of distributed computing? Yeah, easy for you to forget; *not* so for me. Guess what? No sooner did she lay her eyes on Mr. Jowl than her the wayward lectures—your blogger being her captive audience—came to an abrupt halt. My jaw dropped.

It took Ms. Owl a scant few moments, perhaps less, to flutter right over to Mr. Jowl's side and perch herself demurely on the front-right tire of his oh-so-stylish Go-mobile. Well, what do you know! Mr. Jowl, our gopher, is looking positively giddy: Now we got ourselves *two* smitten creatures; not a moment too soon, either. I mean, my neck—if anyone cares about such mundane matters—has somehow gotten spared.

I'm getting out of their merry way. That's for sure.

The two cuties have already vowed fidelity to each other, and plan to get married soon (*Definitely* before the next, annual GopherCon rolls around). Clearly, this is a boon for your blogger, and he readily agrees to keep an eye on the two; a small price to pay.

Yo, I heave a *monumental* sigh of relief, mopping sweat from my brow, realizing the bullet I have dodged. Whew!

The happy couple—and I invite you to come visit them, *and* me, the next time you swing through Austin—have since become permanent residents in my study (I serve as their unwitting chaperone. Oh well).

Now Ms. Owl lectures her beloved Mr. Jowl on stuff such as the best practices for building micro-services; more recently, I'm started hearing them excitedly exchange ideas on the ins and outs of Domain-Driven Design, aka DDD; but that's *only* when Ms. Owl isn't lecturing Mr. Jowl on getting his act together and stop speeding around in his spiffy Go-mobile.

The way I see it, better *him* than me.

And *that's* how I've recently been seeing the world (through the eyes of a gopher, of course).

◆ ◆ ◆

CONGRATULATIONS!
YES
you
Microservices IN ACTION
Microservices Patterns
Version Control with Git
GOPHERCON 2019
Akram Ahmad
Go Web Programming
Google Cloud
GC19
Go Programming Blueprints - Second Edition
JOIN US NEXT TIME...

CHAPTER 3: WORKING MEMORY FOR THE WORKING PROGRAMMER

We are made wise not by the recollection of our past, but by the responsibility for our future.
- George Bernard Shaw

0. Intro

Check that crumpled-looking scratchpad in the pic above—the one impaled by a red paperclip even as it gets singled out by Adam Smith's "invisible hand"—hovering above our wonderstruck lad's head? Ah yes, right there we have the essence of the wonders (and attendant befuddlement) that accompany any mention of this critter called "working memory".

Brah, I wasn't kidding either when I called out the "scratchpad metaphor" in the same breath as working memory. But we're getting ahead of ourselves (If you truly can't help yourself—curiosity is getting the better of you—then look up why it's cool to find out more about our mental scratchpad.)

Oh, did I tell you about the fine researcher-lad Alan Baddeley's use of the metaphor dealing with a company boss to describe the way in which the central executive operates? So...

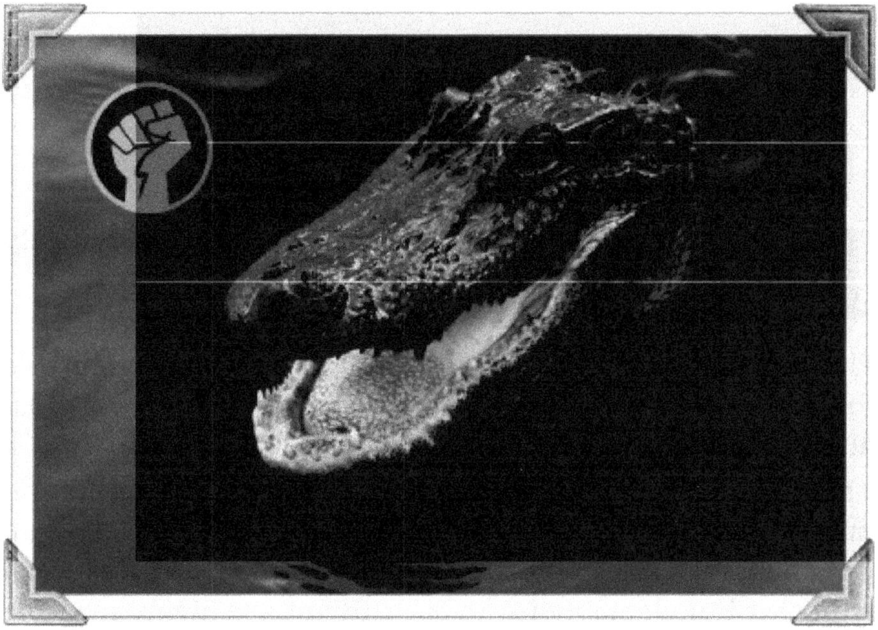

1. Hey, Come Back!

Don't run away. At least, not quite yet. We've barely begun, you know.

Plus we're talking *crucial* stuff here. Stuff that's indispensable for carrying out knowledge work; basically, the stuff that most all of us do nowadays, most all of the time.

As related to those of us who are practitioners of the art of computer programming, check what legendary Lisp hacker Paul Graham has to say about working memory—the foundational stuff that it undeniably is—in his brilliant and highly readable book *Hackers & Painters...*

For a bit more—and we really should let Paul Graham complete his thought—let's turn to that giant house of cards which is on the verge of tottering.

Check this. KABOOM!

KABOOM!

2. GOOD ENOUGH FOR NOW, YEAH?

Cool. I, too, think it is.

(Warning: Don't try that playing cards experiment at home. At least not quite yet; those innocuous looking cards might slice through your hands like machete blades. Okay, okay, *just* kidding. Some people ain't got no sense of humor. Sheesh!)

So let's move on to more serious business, such as railway tracks. All aboard.

3. All Aboard (For Some Erudition)

If you want to build a ship, don't drum up people to collect wood and don't assign them tasks and work, but rather teach them to long for the endless immensity of the sea.
- Antoine de Saint-Exupery

Such erudition on display in those trenchant lines of verse. So complete a mastery of the railroad jargon. Oh my!

Yep, that can't be beat. Jujitsu style, though, let's take in the pic—the one right above the verses of rhyme—and focus on the conjoining and switching among the mesh of railroad tracks.

That's right. We cook up, let's say, an algorithm in our head, adding in the details, bit by bit—thimbleful by thimbleful. It's in the switching between contexts that we programmers make gold, if you will allow a wee digression into the story of King Midas and his touch.

Hey, did anyone even notice the pachyderm—that's simply an elephant, for folks like you and I—which I had surreptitiously planted alongside the railroad tracks? (Yo, come to think of it, does anyone ever notice the dainty borders that I put around the pics in essays such as this one and which, needless to say, I cull from the public domain?)

Anyhow, with a cranium the size of an elephant, that lumbering dude must have an enormous working memory? Conjectures ahoy. Anyone.

4. Behold The Bezier-Mesh Cranium

People always complain about their memories, never about their minds.
- Francois de La Rochefoucauld

Anyhow, and setting conjectures (about elephants boasting enormous working memory) aside for a minute, a ton of scientific studies have dissected the workings of working memory six different ways.

Oh yes. And prominent among them is the work of Philip Johnson-Laird—for an engaging account of (some of those) scientific studies, I can recommend that you look up his fine book entitled *How We Reason* (Oxford University Press).

Hey, did anyone even *notice* the button hovering above the bezier mesh cranium in the pic above—along with a flaming red cookout barbecue on the grounds—which is to symbolize *The Curious Case of Benjamin Button*, a witty and fantastical satire about aging (with the accompanying effects of the passage of time on memory.) Oh yeah, while that guy F. Scott Fitzgerald is mostly known for his novels, he sure knew how to spin a yarn, too.

Wait. We're not doing Lit; at least not right now, since we did it back then.

Meanwhile, you feeling adventurous enough to upload new skills *directly* to the brain? Just like in the film *The Matrix*, using those plug-and-play cartridges (check the pic below.) Aha, let's see what this hopping, little bird has to tell us...

PATRIOT
8GB
SDx10
SDHC SD
Memory Card / Carte Mémoire
8 GB GO

5. Memories Are Made Of This

Human memory is about to get supercharged. Or is it? I mean, are you ready to upload new skills directly to your splendid cranium, just like in the film The Matrix? I *bet* you are, considering the plentiful demands on your copious, free (!) time:

- Figured out yet the sequence of operations that make the Gorilla multiplexer tick?
- Unraveled the mysterious art of keeping those dainty algorithms loaded in your memory?
- Had a reckoning with the glory (ignominy, perhaps) of resource contention?
- Oh, and you got the unfolding chain of eventual consistency down pat, right?

What is that you say? Ah, good, so you're going to take a number and get in line for your very own upload of skills straight to your cantankerous cranium.

And should you wish to pursue this even further—in the spirt of how The future is already here; it's just not evenly distributed ala William Gibson—then you owe it to yourself to read up on this article at *NewScientist* about how *Matrix*-style memory prosthesis is set to supercharge the human brain.

Nice.

POOF!

6. Strolling Down Memory Lane

The accompanying pic of the stroll itself will, I hope—in the spirit of the vaunted Reader's Digest monthly column Toward More Picturesque Speech—suffice to paint a complete picture.

Enough said.

7. Incipient Memories

We are now, shall we say, no longer on terra firma (aka "here be dragons".) Check the memory vortex above: Methinks this is looking more and more like a lurching lunge into the dungeon of nascent memories, something right out of the harrowing movie Incipient.

Speaking of which, and according to an AI-focused issue of *The MIT Technology Review* (Oct 26, 2018), a controversial artwork created by the juggernaut that is AI hauled in $435,000 at an auction. That's a *lot* of dollars, if you ask me, for a mere lunge into the workings of working memory!

Dollars or no, *I'm* out of here before I get swallowed by that harrowing dungeon: AARGH!

8. Trouble, On Tentacles

Row row row your boat,
Gently down the stream.
If you see a crocodile,
Don't forget to scream.
~ *Row, Row, Row Your Boat* (a popular, nursery rhyme)

Yeah boy—yes, that's you, faux gondolier, suspenders and all—while you're busy pointing out to your unsuspecting gondola-bearing guests the blithering and slithering deep sea angler fish that has surfaced (likely checking out the newly-opened strip mall along the leafy banks of the fine River Thames), do you mind turning your head to the other side of your gondola?

Yikes. The "green-eyed monster" itself! Come to think of it, it's all green, and not very friendly either.

Yeah, brah, I was trying to tell ya: We got moh trouble at starboard.

And this ain't our friendly, tentacled mascot from EdgeX either.

That's why I keep telling you (and myself!) that it's good to learn how to chew gum *and* walk at the same time. And while you juggle the implications furiously—we're trying to save our imperiled lives here, in case you didn't notice—let me point you to the finest when it comes to reaping the results of searching high and low for the gestalt of working memory:

The Ravenous Brain: How the New Science of Consciousness Explains Our Insatiable Search for Meaning by Daniel Bor (Basic Books)

What. A. Book.

ML for the
WORKING
PROGRAMMER
L.C. Paulson
Schlumberger

9. Speak Memory

For anyone still scratching their head, wondering where the unearthly title of this essay—"Working Memory for the Working Programmer"—came from, I can now help. Check the pic above: You'll spy an eminently eco-friendly-green book with the bold title ML for the Working Programmer, a book which I bought many moons ago, back when I was tackling the Cambridge University Press' Purely Functional Data Structures by Chris Okasaki.

But wait... OMG! Is that Ms. *Owl* herself, perched atop our copy of the eco-friendly-green book? Gulp, anyone even remember our adventures when Ms. Owl used to flutter right over to the side of Mr. Jowl—our very own gopher from GopherCon 2019 in San Diego—and perch herself demurely on the front-right tire of his oh-so-stylish Go-mobile.

Well, what do you know! Ms. Owl is back, looking positively giddy. Help!

And we're done. More like, we're done *for*. Or something; *that's* for sure.

Oh, speaking of memory, brownie points for anyone who spots Vladimir Nabokov's *Speak, Memory: An Autobiography* that's suitably anchored, weighed down—inveighed eh, heh heh?—by *ML for the Working Programmer.*

I'm telling you, memory can be elusively sieve-like at times... I turned to look but it was gone, I cannot put my finger on it now. The child's grown, the dream's gone: POOF!

Which is why, of course—what with Sherlock Holmes having bit the dust many moons ago—we're sending for the finest detective services money can buy nowadays. Read on to find out.

10. Send For Our Top Detective

People always complain about their memories, never about their minds.
- Francois de La Rochefoucauld

That would be Monsignor Parrot, of course, suitably disguised to blend in with the natives. Yo, craven Mr. Toucan, how did you flutter into our pic? You're supposed to be overseeing culinary efforts, baking all those cakes and pastries, for crying out loud.

Yeah, you're fetching—or *something*—but can you, like, stay out of hush-hush photos involving sleuth work of the utmost sensitive nature?

◆ ◆ ◆

CHAPTER 4: ON THE UNREASONABLE EFFECTIVENESS OF PATTERNS

0. Intro

There is nothing so absurd that some philosopher has not already said it.
- Cicero

I have this recurring dream in which I'm kneeling down and writing—nay, inscribing—beautiful mathematical equations on the pages of a magisterial volume that I find flung open before me. The equations themselves are in closed form, describing aspects of a mathematical model, inscribed—nay, chiseled—in acutely silhouetted calligraphy inspired by the venerable Maxwell's Equations.

During such dreams, I find the passage of time falling by the wayside. And though you may spy a time-keeping instrument in the pic coming right up, time-keeping is *not* on my mind; it is *patterns* that I am—and soon you, too, will be—after.

Speaking of dreams, though, and that, too, from the vantage point of patterns, I should mention in passing that renowned catalog of sorts, assembled by none other than Sigmund Freud, and known as *The Interpretation of Dreams*.

So dreamers, don't you stop dreaming.

But for now, we'll leave such ethereal pursuits to the time-honored tales that are known to unravel only on a dark and stormy night or two. So yeah, the patterns we'll be chasing are far less elusive and evanescent than the stuff of dreams.

Anyone remember our skirmishes with *Incipient* the last time around? Yes, we need to go deeper.

Let's dig in.

1. Tick Tock, Exploring Patterns Ad Hoc

A man's interest in the world is only the overflow from his interest in himself. When you are a child your vessel is not yet full; so you care for nothing but your own affairs. When you grow up, your vessel overflows; and you are a politician, a philosopher, or an explorer and adventurer. In old age the vessel dries up: there is no overflow: you are a child again.

~ George Bernard Shaw

Regular readers who continue to converge—by means such as stochastic gradient descent or regula falsi—onto our blogging regions here find to their continued delight that we just don't do any boring stuff here. The way my readers and I see it, life is too short to mull over the quotidian. And our foray this time, into patterns, will not be an exception, amirite?

First, though, I need to get something off my chest: As someone who *strongly* identifies with the common man and woman—lest any of the talk around here, heaven forbid, even *begin* to smack of privilege—as someone who has had the privilege of attending (excellent) state universities, I wish to reassure readers that I'm one of *you*. Whew, that confession (aka disclosure) sure felt good!

Okay now, and regardless of your persuasion and sensibilities, I hope you'll agree with Oscar Wilde's assessment to "*Be yourself; everyone else is already taken.*"

But I digress.

Here's where we are headed: We will, together, shortly trek through the land of patterns in a way that's not been done before. One more time, and *all* together now—especially so if you checked out the essay served here last time—we agreed that creativity is a renewable resource. And ain't it?

Hey, what's up with that cluster of gossamer, oh-so-fragile Turkey Tails mushrooms appearing into sight?

2. Exploring Intersections And Gaps

Nature is an infinite sphere of which the center is everywhere and the circumference nowhere.
- Blaise Pascal

Uneasily eying that bunch of gossamer mushrooms for a few moments—as would befit one who can't tell the harmless kind from the poisonous—even a troglodyte like yours truly can discern in their oh-so-elegant arrangement the underlying theme of "intersections and gaps."

Check how those mushrooms' jagged, ragged, and outwardly burgeoning, chocolatey edges overlap, intersect, *even* as they expose gaps?

Reminds me of a fascinating, though brief, chat recently where I heard the view that creativity can be likened to pattern-matching in that cultivating the ability to pore over incongruous data (from disparate sources) and finding patterns in that data can very well lead one to identify intersections and gaps.

It is that gripping perspective which has, in turn, served as the fuel and fire of this exploratory essay.

This stuff—I say we take one more wistful look at those near-diaphanous chocolate-and-vanilla hued mushrooms—is ripe for exploring, *Kit Kat* though it's chocolatey stems definitely are not made of. Shall we put on our mushroom-hunting hats?

First, though, we go *pattern*-hunting; *mushroom*-hunting will have to wait.

Sorry to dash those dreams.

3. A Preview Of Things To Come

With the throat clearing behind us—you know, having talked some about the stuff of dreams, their linkages to patterns, and in remembrance of things past—we've got a bird'e eye view of the terrain coming right up for you.

Here, then, are the signposts for the terrain that follows them:

- We Dive Right In!
- The Pattern On The Stone
- The Science Of Patterns
- Are Patterns Transformative?
- Pattern Recognition Goes To Town
- Patterning Our Lives After Analogies
- Pattern Matching Since Democritus
- Why Humans Hunger For Patterns (And Meaning)
- Mining Patterns (From Incongruous Data)
- Disparate Sources, Unifying Patterns
- Design Patterns, Too, Have Their Day
- A Stack Of Patterns
- Patterns For Creativity And Productivity
- Patterns Everywhere, Untethered, Yet Moored
- Flowing (Carving), Rising (Towering), and Scintillating (Showering)
- Penguins A-Marching To Escarpment Ahoy
- I Had Kneeled To Inscribe Patterns...

With out eyes set on some fun exploration, let's you and I dive right in.

AKRAM AHMAD

Shall we?

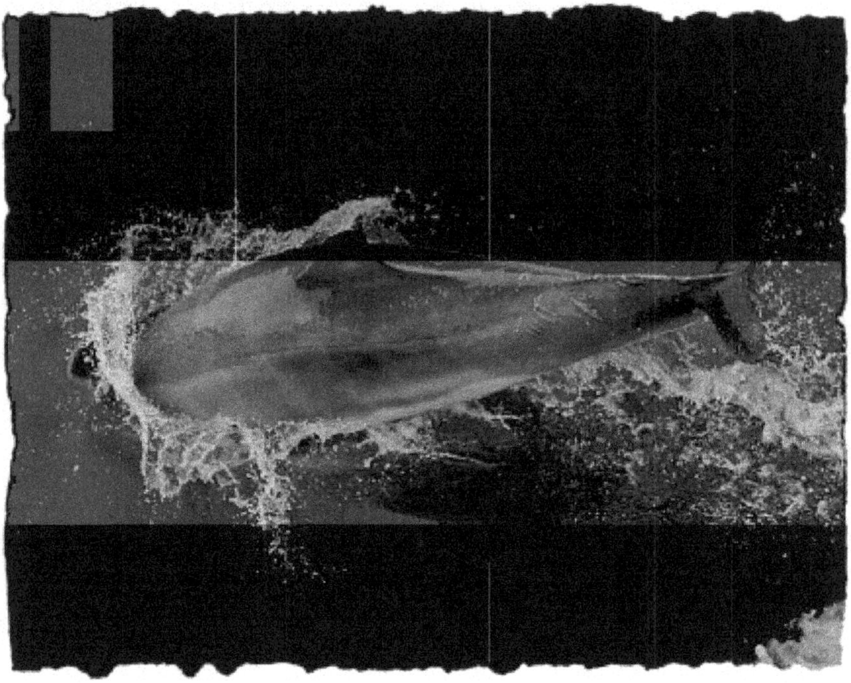

4. We Dive Right In!

At long last, we now have nothing to fear but fear itself—surely your path has crossed at least one of those red-and-white, striped stickers with the shibboleth "NO FEAR" shouting in all caps.

Take comfort, too, in the knowledge that we are leagues away from the environs of the violent thunderstorm that had raged one dark and stormy night in *Cape Fear*. That was one chilling movie; gave me nightmares for weeks. I wouldn't watch it again, even if I were *paid* to do so.

(Sheesh, that movie and others of its ilk, such as the thriller *Silence of the Lambs*, just ain't my thing.)

Goodbye to that thing of the past; it bites the dust. And there it stays.

We're good.

All you and I have to do now is follow the arc of the narrative.

TURING'S VISION THE BIRTH OF COMPUTER SCIENCE
daniel hillis
the pattern on the stone
GO

5. The Pattern On The Stone

What happened here, I asked myself, and what chain of events it was that led to the pattern on the stone finally getting divulged?

From that departure point, it wasn't too much of a stretch to recall the soulful lyrics of piano maestro Elton John when he had voiced a similar question in a song...

So let's start—and ignoring for now that giddy gopher who you'll note in the pic above has commandeered a rather fuzzy gopher mobile—with a brief dip into an elegant book by the name of *The Pattern on the Stone: The Simple Ideas that Make Computers Work* by accomplished computer scientist Danny Hillis, who studied AI under Marvin Minsky and was at one time a protege of the late and great Nobel Prize-winning physicist Richard Feynman after he (i.e. Hillis) had co-founded Thinking Machine Corporation.

The stone that Hillis is referring to—somewhat obliquely through the enigmatic title of his book, *The Pattern on the Stone* —is silicon wafer (aka computer chip), and the patterns etched on the chip as well as the programs that instruct the computer to do this or that and how they (i.e. the instructions) are generated according to a few basic, easily explainable principles.

Computers are arguably the most complex human creation ever. Yet, in a fundamental sense, they are remarkably simple —obediently carrying out orders, ours for now—thanks to the wizardry of the pattern etched into the stone.

But what came *before* computers that enabled computers to gain purchase in the first place? Some scaffolding had to be present. So yeah, what machinery, what perfect storm, was *already* in place that enabled computers to burst into existence?

Hint: That subject—the "machinery" that I just referred to—begins with the first letter of the name of my former state (Minnesota.)

6. The Science Of Patterns

Patterns are everywhere, oh everywhere, and in any subject you care to name, if you know how—and where—to look for them. Nowhere is this truer than for the queen of sciences: Math has been called the science of patterns.

Fancy that.

And if you think I'm making this up, I invite you to cast your gaze upward to the square-center of the pic above, where, for crying out loud, you'll see a *book* by that name: *Mathematics As a Science of Patterns* by Michael D. Resnik (Oxford University Press).

And not only is that fine Resnick book supporting (1) a blue-and-red, spade-wielding Pokémon figurine, and (2) an elegant, London souvenir mug, it (i.e. the Resnick book) is doing double duty by also serving as a (figurative *and* literal) bridge between two broad areas of math—pure (math) on the left, and impure, excuse me, *applied* (math) on the right.

With a setup like that—not that you have to follow me along as I sweat the small stuff in setting up cameos like the one above —it only stands to reason that we might as well have some fun, such as having our Resnick book serve *yet* another purpose (its third, and counting, thereby monotonically veering in the direction of stretching our math ability to its limits, monotonic or otherwise).

Are you tracking me? Am *I* tracking me?

(This is getting so meta.)

Woohoo! The science of patterns—or at least the *book* by that name—is also helping our Pokémon pal and its inseparable cohort (the London mug) whisk over for a slide, taking advantage of the (relative) lopsidedness of the tomes on which the said book squarely rests. Evidently, the purists have a whole lot *more* to say (in *The Princeton Companion to Mathematics*) than their *applied* counterparts (in *The Princeton Companion to Applied Mathematics*).

The proof of how this came to be so is left as an exercise for the reader. (Want to hazard a guess about how many times *I* was on the receiving end of hand-waving back in my school days?)

Joking aside, and lest you think I'm partisan to any (one) branch of math, I have at various times found myself torn between the austere, Dickinsonian beauty of *pure* math on the one hand, and the obscene usefulness of *applied* math (especially linear algebra) on the other.

Forsooth I had begun this section with a flourish, boldly heralding that patterns are everywhere, provided that you care—more like, *dare*—to look for them. Speaking of which, especially the part having to do with daring, *what* in the world is that upcoming Easter Island statue doing on my (faux) mahogany desk?

7. Are Patterns Transformative?

I would love to change the world, but they won't give me the source code.

~ Anonymous

I've heard that one before (about not having access to the source code, and that, too, in this day and age!) For crying out loud, anyone can now get a free account on Github. So whoever you are—behind that "Anonymous" facade of a moniker with which you've betokened yourself—please get your act together. Thank you.

Heh.

In all seriousness, that lovely, ebony book standing bolt upright on my expansive (definitely *not* expensive) mahogany desk in the pic above—sandwiched between the Easter Island stone statue and the AI books with the connect-the-dots-brain-based enneagram ivory dust jacket—has a hilarious remark by its author that is worth checking out!

Okay, even *seriousness* aside for now, including that zinger above from David Deutsch—at once sardonic, witty, and delightful as it is—here's the thing: Our uniquely human patterns, as Deutsch argues in his remarkably elegant book called *The Beginning of Infinity: Explanations That Transform the World*, have in them the genesis of an intimate connection between explaining the world and *controlling* it.

I don't know about you, but any time *I* see the word "control"—take it from someone who took two semesters' worth of Control Engineering theory as an undergraduate back in the day—I have this knee-jerk reaction to start recalling *Nyquist Diagrams* (only *Nyquil* was quicker at making me sleepy), *Root Locus Analysis* (ugh, avoid those like a plague of locusts), and especially those pesky *Bode Plots* (decimating decibels and irresolvable logarithmic logjam which in their wake they brought) and whatnot, plus other forget-me-nots.

Digress, but I do. Yoda-style, too. Don't I? Oh my!

But guess what? The ability to harness explanatory knowledge —and you really should look up Deutsch's *The Beginning of Infinity* to fully grasp the nuances of the argument—gives us humans the power to transform *nature*. Pause for a few moments.

Let that sink in (the notion of gaining the power to mutate *Mother Nature*.)

Gulp.

Remember, though, that universal laws are the "limiting" factor that govern what we humans run up against in our quest to remake the world. Coincidentally, my coworkers and I were discussing *exactly* this line of thinking recently, during a book club meeting.

Great stuff.

8. Pattern Recognition Goes To Town

It is beyond a doubt that all our knowledge that begins with experience.
- Immanuel Kant

Check that dapper figure above in authentic South Korean attire, complete with a gold medallion embossed across its red tunic, looking real sharp (Should you wish to get to know him more intimately, look no further than some fun we had together in exploring The Soul of Edge Computing as well as when we together pored over Microservices In Small Pieces.)

Closer to the subject at hand—patterns, in general, and my recently becoming aware of the fascinating view that "creativity can be likened to pattern-matching," in particular—and if you recall how we had uneasily eyed that burgeoning bunch of gossamer mushrooms, you know the chocolatey kind, we are now delving into a realm with which I have (way) more than a passing familiarity as well as academic training: Machine Learning (ML) and Pattern Recognition (PR).

See how far we've come already in our pattern-hunting trek? Sigh, that *mushroom*-hunting journey will (still) have to wait. Sorry to keep your hopes dashed (Hit me up later, though, if your heart desires such a journey.)

Since we've already broached the theme of how (obscenely) practical linear algebra is—back when we were having some fun with our slip-sliding Pokemon chap, the one with its London souvenir mug in tow, the one who found himself getting whisked across the bridge spanning the chasm between pure math and applied math—let's keep building on that momentum, shall we?

Cool.

And lest your heart began sinking at the prospect (specter?) of a whale-like paragraph (or two) coming our way, let me assure you that no such tidal wave comes our way. *All* I've got coming up for us is a breadcrumb trail (*Look Ma, no hands!*) by way of a far more leisurely—almost *epistolary*—exploration of pattern-hunting.

So yes, to witness how pattern recognition, in the guise of the fancier-sounding phrase "Deep Learning" (DL), has gone to town over the past decade and a half, and, even more importantly, how *you*, too, can ride that wave, I can do no better than share a breadcrumb trail of my own:

- *Best Deep Learning Books (Foundational)*
- *Best Deep Learning Books (Pragmatic)*
- *Best Deep Learning Books (Popular)*

Between the material at the above-mentioned three coordinates, I have a hunch that you'll find plenty to keep you engaged for a while. (As a next step, and to get your hands on the bits and bytes, I can highly recommend that you check out the online *Machine Learning* course offered by Coursera, which comes complete—*at* its completion, appropriately enough—with a certificate for a Stanford University class taught by Professor Andrew Ng, who was formerly with Google and, later, with Baidu and Drive.ai or something.)

We could delve a bit, too, into my own graduate school work involving Pattern Recognition, which I did many moons ago (my research, thesis area, the back-propagation network, and stuff like that while earning my MS). But that might be pushing your patience, and cool though I think that work was.

Onward.

SURFACES AND ESSENCES
DOUGLAS HOFSTADTER
& EMMANUEL SANDER

9. Patterning Our Lives After Analogies

The mathematical facts worthy of being studied are those which, by their analogy with other facts, are capable of leading us to the knowledge of a physical law.
~ Henri Poincare

Hmm... I'm beginning to see a pattern: Recall how we came to learn of the obscene usefulness of applied math as wielded by its mavens versus the austere and rarefied atmosphere occupied by practitioners of pure math.

Is it too much of a stretch to assert that purity and obscenity do not commingle, and never the twain shall meet?

That analogy may be imprecise and my proposed pattern may hold only *so* much water, but here's the thing: When we turn our attention to the relevance and pervasiveness of math throughout the fabric of science, I can't help but draw parallels to, and resonate with, the marvelously erudite and approachable essay by the Hungarian-American theoretical physicist, engineer, *and* mathematician—boy, he must've been one busy guy!—Eugene Wigner. That essay is entitled *The Unreasonable Effectiveness of Mathematics in the Natural Sciences*. Don't miss it.

But recalling the claim that beauty is more than skin deep, how reasonable is it to pattern our *lives* on analogies? And while we may live by the swathe of metaphors that swirl around in our lives—I, for one, never metaphor I didn't like—does it behoove us to take this a step further and wager our very lives on analogies? Plus taking a cue from the book standing upright in the pic above (*Surfaces and Essences: Analogy as the Fuel and Fire of Thinking* by Douglas Hofstadter and Emmanuel Sander), how do we go from surfaces to their essences, peeling back the layers of abstraction, layer by layer, onion-like?

So many rapid-fire questions, and you're like, "*I don't know, Akram—you tell us!*"

Relax.

Remember one thing, one thing only, and everything will be clear: "*All that glitters is not gold.*" Put another way—and you never heard me utter a non sequitur, now did you?—don't trust everything you see.

Running with that gold metaphor, and should you wish to dig deeper into the ore of analogies, look no farther than the book standing upright in the pic above.

Meanwhile, the jury is still out on the reasonableness of patterning our lives on analogies. And were it not for my fear of mallet-toting mobs—presumably comprised chiefly of those who've also been on the receiving end of hand-waving during their school days—I would have added in departing, "*The task of parametrizing the reasonableness, or otherwise, of such patterning is left as an exercise for the reader.*"

But this ain't my first rodeo, to quote the memorable words of a friend; once bitten, twice shy, that's why—things go awry when you get conked on the head (with a mallet) one time *too* many.

QUANTUM
COMPUTING SINCE
DEMOCRITUS

10. Pattern Matching Since Democritus

Nearing the end of our trek, we feel entitled to poetic license as well as a dollop of philosophy that can only be had by commingling the past with the present.

Specifically, we now hark back to the days of the hilarious philosopher named Democritus, whose hilarity led to his world fame and renown as the "laughing philosopher". Go figure.

Speaking of going to figure things out—cheekily tying this all back in with the Gopher mascot in the pic above, my atrophying trophy of sorts from a tech conference I attended in San Diego in 2019—I realize that I've been bold enough to stand upright not one but *two* books in that pic, amirite?

The first of those two delves into the guts of an unmatched pattern-matching tool with roots in the world of programming—loved and loathed in equal parts—and which goes by the plain enough name of "regular expressions." Hah, match *that!*

As for the second of those two featured books, that one endearingly commandeers *quantum computing*, taking it one heartbeat at a time since days of yore, days that bore the imprint of Democritus—you guessed it, the hilarious philosopher we ran into just a minute ago—bringing the narrative arc right up to and even past the era of Mr. T (Alan Turing, of course).

The choice is yours: Venture forth and explore pattern-matching *with* or without regular expressions, *with* or without trawling into quantum computing. Totally up to you.

Either way, don't forget to take a second look at the haunting and ethereal poem atop this section, the one by Emily Dickinson: I must confess that the subject of software concurrency —coordinating computer programs when more than one task can start and complete in overlapping time periods—rose to the fore of my mind as I selected those ineffable verses of Dickinsonian poetry.

But yes, I do digress.

11. Why Humans Hunger For Patterns (And Meaning)

With a deep statement like the one adorning this section—"Why Humans Hunger For Patterns (And Meaning)"—I hope you're not surprised to see not one but two books (plus actually a third, supine one hiding in plain sight) make an appearance.

And never you mind that whopper of a burger up there in the marquee announcing this section's title.

The layered burger sure is a sight to behold. But you're not *that* hungry.

Or are you?

Hey, before you dash for the nearest fast-food drive-through, can we get some stuff down?

Stuff such as the first featured book, named *Geometry and Meaning,* by Dominic Widdows (Stanford University's Center for the Study of Language and Information), and which is a delectable treat, marrying the worlds of language, math, and search with a delightful geometrical slant.

And the second one is named *The Ravenous Brain: How the New Science of Consciousness Explains Our Insatiable Search for Meaning,* by Daniel Bor (Basic Books). If you want to explore, among other things, the role that our working memory plays in our lives, look no further! Human hunger for finding patterns and meaning-making, too, is tackled splendidly.

As for the third one—*Mathematics As a Science of Pattern-s* by Michael D. Resnik (Oxford University Press)—I invite you to stay tuned; more on that one coming up soon.

Promise.

Patterns of Software
Machine Learning
A Probabilistic Perspective
Kevin P. Murphy

12. Mining Patterns (From Incongruous Data)

Look at that! Our Pokemon pal in his nerdy red jumper, still toting his bright yellow spade, and he sure has the audacity to wink and grin at the same time. Didn't they outlaw that or something?

Anyhow, having recently witnessed our pal's escapades—surely you haven't forgotten about his daring slides across that bookish bridge spanning two distinct math terrains?—authorities are keeping an eye on him, alerting the kingdom far and wide.

Such an alert, in fact, you can spy if you squint at the upright, olive ruler flanking our Pokemon pal above: Notice how it says (that, too, in all caps) that the surface is "NON-SKID"?

OK pal, no more capers now. *You* stay put. No more back-breaking slides on my mahogany desk. You got that, buddy? Leave that sort of thing to other, more-athletic folks. Someone like Megan Rapinoe. And someone like you, of course, dear Reader. *I* sure don't need any OSHA lawsuits on my hands; like others, I, too, got enough on my hands these days, dealing with the unique challenges of COVID-19 (Ever tried giving yourself a haircut? So yeah.)

Anyhow, turning now to the subject of how one can find patterns from disparate sources, which, in turn, can lead one to explore intersections and gaps—an original perspective to which I was recently introduced—is a subject which could have (in fact, *has*) filled books.

Gotta tell ya: That book which stands *upright* in the pic above—*Machine Learning: A Probabilistic Perspective* by Kevin P. Murphy (The MIT Press)—is pure eye candy. Don't get me wrong: It's got the heft to match the most hard-core, technical textbooks out there. But it's so lavishly illustrated (to a fault, if you ask *me*, though nobody does that sort of thing much anymore) that you could be excused for gawking at the multifaceted way in which (ML) beauty is captured in its pages. Great stuff!

And as for the fine book specimen that lies *supine*, again, in the same pic—*Patterns of Software: Tales from the Software Community* by Richard Gabriel (Oxford University Press)—you'll find nary a single picture (or drawing) adorning its pages. But... And this is a *big* but: It is razor-sharp with cutting insights (into where our programming community has been, as where we're headed) like you will likely not find anywhere else. This guy is (*was?*) a hard-core Lisp hacker, belonging to the generational of one of my all-time programming heroes, Guy Steele.

But I digress.

And as I come out of the egress—check the scene coming up, evidently London town re-created right there on my mahogany desk—I spy a quaint, flaming-red telephone booth.

And the next thing I know, I find myself blurting out, "*Operator, can you please place a telephone call for me?*"

This ain't no scene out of *The Matrix*.

Yo, Neo.

Darn, he hung up (Methinks that villainous Cipher dude made Neo do that.)

THE BEST
AMERICAN
ESSAYS
CENTURY
JOYCE CAROL OATES
THE
BEGINNING
OF
INFINITY
DAVID DEUTSCH
LONDON

13. Disparate Sources, Unifying Patterns

Whether or not you peg the scientific revolution to the Enlightenment, the value of patterns and the transformative nature shines through. Much, too much, to lend itself to condensing.

Let's give it a shot, though, and see if we can tease out the essence of how disparate sources can, if properly approached, (eventually) yield unifying patterns.

And now please allow me to explain what that *other*, splendid book—*The Best American Essays of the Century*, edited by the wildly talented and uber-prolific Joyce Carol Oates—is doing in the same pic. It is, in a nutshell, home to essays patterned after the melting pot that is America.

Check it out. You won't be disappointed.

14. Design Patterns, Too, Have Their Day

Everything popular is wrong
- Oscar Wilde

Design patterns, oh, good old design patterns. Where would we be without them. Plus so much has been written about them that if I so much as start to squeak, I have the sneaking suspicion that I'll be shown the door. Kind of like the Elton John joke where he claimed that as a youngster he used to get kicked out of the music room as soon as he started singing Ring a Ring o' Roses.

But this is important stuff; no surprises then that not one or two, but *three* books stand tall (in the pic above) as they testify to how the elemental force of design patterns rocked our software industry. Right up there with a tsunami, albeit a benign one; a tsunami that nourished rather than demolished what lay in its path, regardless of the shores its waves crashed on. In other words, it was a tide—albeit a massive one—that lifted all boats unlike any other our industry had seen before, amirite?

In full candor, another dozen-plus books—on design patterns as well—are orbiting *somewhere* under the rooftop of my house. They all simply wouldn't fit on my mahogany desk, which is why I didn't even attempt to pluck them out of their orbital paths.

And since we were chatting about tsunamis, it gladdens my heart to witness two amigos riding some kind of tsunami—goodness, made up entirely of books!—yet not a drop of water is in sight.

Let's check it.

Go
Cloud Computing
Design Patterns
Design Patterns
Gamma • Helm
Johnson • Vlissides
MACHINE LEARNING
DAVID DEUTSCH
TURING'S VISION
Ravenous Brain
Mathematics

15. A Stack Of Patterns

"And hast thou slain the Jabberwock?
Come to my arms, my beamish boy!
O frabjous day! Callooh! Callay!""
He chortled in his joy.
~ Lewis Carroll (in his utterly serious poem entitled *Jabberwocky*)

So have we done it? That is, have we emulated the beamish boy who slays the terrifying Jabberwocky, apocryphal or otherwise, the one that Lewis Carroll had limned in the hilarious verses above? Put another way, have we sliced in half the Gordian Knot of comprehending patterns in all their varieties?

Oh my, we got another kind of Gordian Knot (of sorts) mushrooming and rising before us like a tidal wave!

And if isn't the dynamic trio this time, with *two* of them riding that wave, and the *one* solemnly keeping vigil on ground:

1. That slip-sliding Pokemon chap, our pal who could not be pried away from its cohort, the London souvenir mug
2. Our ebullient gopher who's evidently still very much in charge of that nifty gopher mobile.
3. The dapper South Korean figurine, complete with his gold medallion and red tunic, looking sharp as ever.

I ask, oh yes, I *do* ask, "*What kind of symbolism does our motley crew have up their sleeves?*" Plus it's only fair to inquire, "*Which leitmotif lies in the lurch of that towering stack of books, lurking for unsuspecting passersby on whom to crash?*" And last, but certainly not least, "*Where...?!!*"

At that moment, the lights went out. The last thing I recall (before the lights went out) was a mallet-like projectile accelerating rapidly in the direction of my cranium. When I came to, I realized that the projectile, now lying beside me, *was* a mallet.

Clearly, my effusive line of questioning, endearing to its bone —oh-so nascent, too—was cut off prematurely upon not being received with *quite* the warmth that the line of questioning deserved.

Rubbing my bleary eyes, I groggily remember the care I had lavished on arranging that towering—though *now*-tottering—stack of books in a "foundational" way, meaning that at the base of it all would be a book about the science of patterns (math, pure and unsullied), above it, one on the stuff inside our cranium, on *its* shoulders (or back, if you wish to view it that way, with its spine demurely jutting outward toward us) standing (actually, sitting) the tome by Hofstadter on going from surfaces to their essences, and so on, as we ascend the stack—book by book—right up until we reach the shiny new book that's a snapshot of our modern world, at least as much as its *digital* infrastructure (cloud computing and such) is concerned.

And with that, I say we call it a wrap, having valiantly slain the Jabberwocky. Let's dial down and take a wok, walk, er, ewok—*something*—over to the shores of those unfathomable seas: creativity and productivity.

Deep Thinking
MICHALKO
CRACKING CREATIVITY
The Productive Programmer
Ford

16. Patterns For Creativity And Productivity

Here's the thing. Creativity and productivity are vast and labyrinthine subjects, so we can at best hope to make a tiny dent.

Here's my proposal:

- For a fuller story on creativity, that ever-elusive chimera, I invite you to check out *The Tao of Creativity*
- And for the lowdown on productivity, how about you check *Working Memory for the Working Programmer*?

With those two resources under your belt, you may well find yourself transformed into a latter-day Leonardo da Vinci, in which case I implore you to remember yours truly, *especially* when you become rich and famous.

Deal?

17. Patterns Everywhere, Untethered, Yet Moored

Everywhere, oh everywhere, untethered, yet moored. That's the magic of patterns in all their varieties, great and small.

I do confess, though, that this section owes its existence to serving as a parking spot for those serene verses from perhaps the finest poet the world has witnessed so far.

To take up the vernacular, she be lightin' the way for future generations of writers—those crafting verses of poetry as well as those crafting lines of prose—in a way no sista' (or brutha', for that matter) ever done before, amirite?

18. Flowing (Carving), Rising (Towering), and Scintillating (Showering)

I have no special talent. I am only passionately curious.
- Albert Einstein

Another confession—regarding this penultimate section as well as the next—is in order.

In prepping this essay, I had assembled a boatload of pictures that I simply couldn't bring myself to jettison off. Most of those pics—the ones peppering the sections appearing earlier this essay—thankfully found their homes.

As for the remaining handful, you guessed it: They were disconsolate, pining for a home. And home is where the heart is, amirite? So we came through with the art of the heart that is this ragtag collage.

And I had gone bleary eyed, just to get those edges, the jagged ones around the collage each—not to mention the pictures accompanying the earlier sections—serrated *just* right, *oh*-so-right; please don't tell me you didn't even notice.

Gah.

Finally, sigh, and if you could please turn you gaze upward, just past the solemn scientific theory doubtless promulgated by a travel-weary (and possibly stranded) airline traveler. Yes, *right* there, that collage of three pictures. Starting from the leftmost one, and going clockwise:

1. Notice the patterns those whorls make in the sand. Does that remind you of the magical feeling when you

first saw tree rings?

2. See that staid, red-brick building rising into the sky, encompassed by a more contemporary, steel-and-glass structure. Does the selfsame pattern perhaps remind you of how we encapsulate objects?
3. The fiery streak lighting up the nighttime sky, illuminating the horizon or brightly down the benighted backdrop? Notwithstanding the coolness of the Doppler Effect—anyone remember the jarring change in pitch in a passing siren, or perhaps the redshift seen by astronomers?—does this pattern remind you of how the strength of a sound signal is strongest near its *source,* rarefying outward?

What is it that you say? "*Hey Akram, can you, like, stop yammering so we can at least enjoy the lovely collages in peace?*", I think I heard you say.

Darn. I'm outta here.

Pronto.

19. Penguins A-Marching To Escarpment Ahoy

Folks, my lips are sealed. From here on, it's just you and the gorgeous collages.

I ain't going near no railroad crossing, let alone that jaundiced sign for a *penguin* crossing. No sir, and no madam. *Oh* no.

And those intricate patterns carved by the waters—or was it the wind?—which you'll surely spy in the escarpment above, don't even get me *started*...

Yo, what's up with those bright-green, feathery fronds ahoy?

20. I Had Kneeled

To Inscribe Patterns...

The difficulty is to try and teach the multitude that something can be true and untrue at the same time.
- Arthur Schopenhauer

Curtain call. Yes. It's that time.

We began our trek with my recurring dream in which I'm kneeling down to inscribe mathematical equations on the pages of a grand volume, a thing of splendor, the equations reminiscent of the glorious—and paradigm-shifting—Maxwell's Equations.

Having come full circle, we now turn to Nature for another dollop of inspiration. Yet again, and much as we've done throughout history, wisp of a sliver though our history is, viewed from the *unvarnished*, grand perspective of the universe.

Speaking of grandness, look who we got assembled below for curtain call: Luminaries from the patterns firmament. Each luminary with a unique story to tell, amirite?

Your lips move, dear luminaries, but I can't hear what you say. And don't you *all* speak at the same time.

Crickets. *Now* I could hear a pin drop.

Darn.

If it ain't one thing, it's another. O brother.

You come back next time; we'll have this sorted out by then.

I think...

◆ ◆ ◆

Go

CHAPTER 5: BEST JAVA BOOKS (2020)

0. Intro

An unfulfilled vocation drains the color from a man's entire existence.
- Honore de Balzac

Which fountain of youth it bathed in will likely remain shrouded in mystery during our lifetimes, this polyglot programmer all the same is amazed by how this one programming language, the one we'll be talking about in this essay—Java, as you may tell by the mound of coffee beans coming right next up—has defied aging unlike any other language you care to name. It's been around for decades, and, like the Energizer Bunny, is still going strong.

And yes, Java isn't *that* old: the horse-drawn buggy in the picture above doesn't quite accurately reflect the year—or even the century, come to think of it—when Java arrived on the scene. Considerations of antiquity aside, this programming language landed like a tsunami and turned our industry upside-down. Who could've predicted *that?*

So it is that many of us in the trenches have used Java to great effect. It sure has taken us on *quite* the ride. In this essay, then, we're going to check out some of the finest learning resources to help our ride that much smoother, and take us to the threshold of yet more frontiers as they open up. Smitten enough for now? Good.

But why in the world would I, as I did, put that electrifying Honore de Balzac quote atop this essay? Well, for one thing, forget all about *The Great Gatsby* (and its attendant big city lights) and please focus, if you please could, on the import of Honore de Balzac opining how "*An unfulfilled vocation drains the color from a man's entire existence.*"

The answer to *exactly* that is coming right next up, following a complementary cup of Java, which I've set daintily atop a sea of coffee beans; hey, I even checked their origins and they sure weren't *Spring beans*—so yeah, we're talking about the edible stuff here.

1. It All Began With A Cup Of Java

What would life be without coffee? But then, what is it even with coffee?
~ King Louis XV

Now that you've had a few reviving sips of your Java, let me spill the beans, the beans, and nothing but the beans: So the reason I quoted Fitzgerald was that, for one thing—and taking a cue here from the adage that "a wealth of information creates a poverty of attention"—our attention spans nowadays are fickle. So anything I can do to help you (and me) perk up a bit can only help.

Really, though, here's the deal: As polyglot programmers, we context-switch between different styles—and even paradigms—as we move from programming in one language to programming in another. To take the example of some languages I'm most familiar with, writing code in Go is a vastly different experience when compared to writing code in Java, which, in turn, is measurably different, in both kind and degree, from hacking Scala code.

Oh, and if my use above of the word "paradigms" struck you as hyperbole, allow me to quote on good authority—none less than Alan Perlis, the Yale computer scientist who became the first ever recipient of the Turing Award—that "*A language that doesn't affect the way you think about programming, is not worth knowing.*"

And then we can go meta with, but of course, the headiness of paradigm blending. But I digress.

And while I confess not knowing much (at all) about the origins of such statements as the hilarious pontification above on all things coffee by King Louis XV—who would've thought that kings, other than *King Ralph* of course, could be so funny?—as only regality would deign to sprinkle around like confetti, I can vouch for the need to have some caffeinated beverage at hand to help power us through the remainder of this essay.

Actually, we're just getting *started*. Yep, we're talking Java—mocha latte.

Cool beans?

2. Ducks In A Row

Admiration for a quality or an art can be so strong that it deters us from striving to possess it.
- Friedrich Nietzsche

So I sat down and began whittling down my list of wannabe-in-this-essay books—oh yeah, I kept paring away—until I had it down to something digestible. Look, I don't want to unwittingly make my readers get a case of indigestion by, say, serving up an unpalatably generous offering, and, in turn, having them groan and reach for that blue Maalox bottle tucked away in their medicine closet.

Well, pared down to the essence, here, then, are the books—like ducks in a row—which were left standing after the dust from my frenzied whittling had settled:

1. ***Growing Object-Oriented Software, Guided by Tests*** by Steve Freeman and Nat Pryce (Addison-Wesley Professional)
2. ***Effective Java, 3rd Edition*** by Joshua Bloch (Addison-Wesley Professional)
3. ***Java Concurrency in Practice*** by Brian Goetz et al (Addison-Wesley Professional)
4. ***Modern Java Recipes: Simple Solutions to Difficult Problems in Java 8 and 9*** by Ken Kousen (O'Reilly Media)
5. ***Effective Unit Testing*** by Lasse Koskela (Manning Publications)
6. ***Java in a Nutshell: A Desktop Quick Reference, 6th Edition*** by David Flanagan and Benjamin Evans (O'Reilly Media)

Before we review each one, in turn, all the while keeping an eye on what makes every one of these sparklers uniquely valuable to you in your journey to mastering Java, let's make a quick pit stop. Actually, I confabulated a bit: As it turns out, it's not quite a pit stop that we'll be making. Folks, we've came to a *fork* in the road.

What's up with that?

Oh, and I haven't told you about a recent, inspiring conversation —one that has rendered the signal service of being the fuel and fire that made this essay happen—a conversation which ran the gamut from the science of quantum computing to the art of blogging to the pragmatics of working remotely to going meta?

Meanwhile, do just one thing for me, won't you please? Keep your eyes peeled for a guest appearance of Schrödinger's cat. Yep, Schrödinger's, not mine—*my* feisty feline, all his tangerine loveliness, goes by the name Lumos.

But I digress.

3. We Came To A Fork

Nature knows no pause in progress and development, and attaches her curse on all inaction.
-Johann Wolfgang von Goethe

Not taking the advice of the wisecrack (evidently also an unrepentant subscriber to the philosophy that finders are keepers) who once said, "When you come to a fork in the road, take it", we tried instead to use the fork (Harking back to Jedi Master Yoda's timeless advice, which he had solemnly dispensed to Luke Skywalker in the immortal words, "Use the fork, Luke, use the fork").

However, not quite finding the fork palpably present—sigh, it wasn't *as* corporeal as we had hoped for it to be—we decided to "fork" it, having once been, way back in the day, diligent students of operating systems.

Wait, come back! I can't stand the sight of all those tears rolling down your cherubic cheeks. It's just that some of us here couldn't resist tossing in some geek humor. Sheesh, that was all.

Plus a little bird tells me that I should discreetly drop my plan of regaling you in the fascinating world wherein dwell such phantasmagorical beasts as—surely you remember the recent talk and such of my cat Lumos, um, actually—*Schrödinger's* cat making a guest appearance?

Let's fork all that to later—have it run as a background process meanwhile—until it's time to bring it right back to the foreground. Did I really say that? Yikes (Channeling Schrödinger's cat may be next, judging by the way things are going).

Seriously, though, Java the *language*—and the Java *ecosystem* even more so—has come to many a fork in the road over the years, and handled it with aplomb, scarcely ever careening or, heaven-forbid, skidding. Most recently, bowing to the wishes of the legions of Java programmers for functional programming features, a tip of the hat to the shepherds of Java for pulling off the introduction of just such features into the language proper. Sweet!

4. Book #1: On Growing (Java) Software

Mary, Mary, quite contrary
How does your garden grow?
~ Mother Goose (in the one-and-only *Mary, Mary, Quite Contrary*)

If inspiration is what you're after—say, to power your very next programming jag—copious amounts thereof can be found between the covers of Growing Object-Oriented Software, Guided by Tests by Steve Freeman and Nat Pryce (Addison-Wesley Professional). Published to great acclaim, this book is suffused with code commentary of the highest caliber.

So yes, if pure inspiration is what you seek—high octane, too, at that—give this gem a read. And yeah, should my plaudits strike you as a bit effusive, I have to level with you and divulge the sentiment that we all in the trenches do get carried away once in a while. But I'm telling you, inspiration and quality, beautiful code go hand-in-hand.

Having made that rather audacious claim—touching as it did on beautiful code—and in the process having opened the proverbial Pandora's box, I owe you a fuller explanation. But not having enough real estate left in this section, allow me to point you in the direction of some musings entitled *Beautiful Code, Beautiful Prose*.

So let's see, why don't we next take a page from that perennial bestseller, *The 7 Habits of Highly Effective People*, and do the same here (for Java, of course).

LIVE
Joshua Bloch
Effective Java
Third Edition

5. Book #2: On Being Effective

Style is effectiveness of assertion.
~ George Bernard Shaw

This is simply an excellent book, with a decidedly pragmatic outlook; all stuff, no fluff. And what with my having a background in electrical engineering, I couldn't help but reflexively think to the notion of the Signal-to-Noise Ratio (aka SNR). So yeah, the SNR in the contents of Effective Java 3rd Edition by Joshua Bloch (Addison-Wesley Professional) is about as high as it gets.

So it is no surprise that this book, very rightly, is just about as highly referenced compendium of Java wisdom as can be found on our fragile planet. Treat this book with care—much as I know that you lavish our planet with care—and tend to it carefully. You will be repaid in (Java) wisdom, many times over.

Organized into bite-sized topics, each one covering a crucial aspect of the sprawling landscape that makes up the juggernaut that is Java, the treatment of each topic is substantial nonetheless. The effect is great. You'll be effective in no time, amirite?

Don't miss this one.

BRIAN GOETZ
JAVA
CONCURRENCY
IN PRACTICE

6. Book #3: Taming Concurrency

Time destroys the speculation of men, but it confirms nature.
- Cicero

If you're going to write a pile of Java code, make sure to have at your side a copy of this age-defying gem of a book. This marvelous book is another keeper. And oh my, how well Java Concurrency in Practice by Brian Goetz et al (Addison-Wesley Professional) has aged since it was published in 2005.

It has somehow managed to take a page from the queen of sciences—so it's been said about math that it never goes out of style—this book on the crucial topic of concurrency is showing (15 years after its publication) hardly any signs of aging. Wow, that's unheard of in an industry where entire *paradigms* shift under us within half a decade!

Incredibly well-edited, and crystal-clear in exposition, this fine volume is quite the expose and remains the go-to source for taming the world of multi-core processors in which we all dwell now. Remember, it all goes back to the basics: How to slay that red-eyed complexity monster, you know the one that has taken one redeye flight too many? Seriously, though—and if you'll humor me by taking this one on faith— conquer concurrency is to slay that red-eyed complexity monster, amirite?

This book will arm you well to slay complexity in the world of Java.

LIVE
O'REILLY
Modern
Java Recipes

7. Book #4: Cooking With Gas (And Java)

No profit grows where is no pleasure taken;
In brief, sir, study what you most affect.
~ William Shakespeare (in *The Taming of the Shrew*)

And when you're ready to cook, we got you covered, too. If you're anything like me, and learn best from tons of examples, then run and grab your very own copy—or someone else's, if they let you have their's—of Modern Java Recipes: Simple Solutions to Difficult Problems in Java 8 and 9 by Ken Kousen (O'Reilly Media)

It's written in the tradition of your typical cookbook—think algorithmic and to-the-point. What sets it apart from its competitors is the pleasing coherence and unity which runs uniformly through the entire narrative.

Oh yes, while we are on the topic of algorithms, I would be remiss if I didn't point you in the direction of two additional resources:

- A pile of the best in the realm of algorithmic goodness
- A second serving of wisdom in the land of algorithms

How are we doing? Plenty of reading material for now? All "booked up", eh, as they say. Good, let's move on from the pragmatics of cookbook-style algorithms to an even more pragmatic aspect of programming (in Java).

Effective
UNIT TESTING

8. Book #5: On The Unbearable Lightness Of Feedback

Trust, but verify.
~ Popular proverb

Tell me if you've heard this one before: "Unit testing is the rigor of software." If memory serves me right, I came across this memorable phrase while reading The Productive Programmer by Neil Ford, many moons ago. Doing admirable justice to this vital topic is on display through the length and breadth of this book.

Ignore the pragmatics offered in *Effective Unit Testing* by Lasse Koskela (Manning Publications) at your own peril.

If you're thinking what *I* think *you* may be thinking—like, reading up on testing has got to be as boring as watching crabgrass grow—this book stands an excellent chance of disproving exactly such an assumption.

Yo, on top of all that, if ever you thought that a programming book couldn't possibly read like an adventure, be prepared to have your mind changed in that department as well. Yep, this is one terrific book.

LIVE
O'REILLY
Java
in a Nutshell
Benjamin J. Evans & David Flanagan

9. Book #6: Tempest In A Teapot

In a nutshell, that is, within the minimalist confines of the shell of a nut—your choice, physical or figurative—decades of (Java) programming wisdom has been condensed for your consumption. Thus it is that, occupying the space between the two covers of Java in a Nutshell: A Desktop Quick Reference 6th Edition by David Flanagan and Benjamin J Evans (O'Reilly Media), you'll find a wealth of knowledge.

David Flanagan, the principal author who kicked off this series of indispensable books—now into its ninth edition—is one amazing writer. A graduate of MIT, he is *quite* the writer: His books are uniformly brilliant, marvels of clarity and grace. The one we are talking about, which is all about what makes Java tick, is no exception.

All the stuff, without any fluff, this book's a winner, well worth your time to at least check out, if not to devour outright. Watch out, T-Rex.

10. Watch 'Em Grow

Like the fork in the road that we came to earlier—I'll wait for you here while you dutifully scroll up to the length of this essay to check it out again— what happened next was like déjà vu all over again for me. I'll go out on a limb and say: Your nice, organized lives as readers may never quite have prepared you to fathom the trouble we writers go to so as to serve you.

But that's enough of *me*. Here, then, was the dilemma: What I had on my hands was not one but *two* fabulous quotes—one drawn from prose, the other from verse. How to keep one and, thus, drop the other, gaah!

Help.

Channeling Schrödinger's cat in my desperation or, for that matter, my own cat Lumos to stand and deliver. Yo, wherefore art thou? Someone. *Anyone?*

Yay, the theme of duality makes yet another appearance and saves the day. Oh yeah, and as you might have noticed, while every other section is embroidered with a solitary quote, who said anything about this section having one quote too many?—*two*, to be precise.

Right, so Java the language began life as *Oak*. Forget nutshells. *Oak* it was. And oh my, how it grew, *and* grew—*Jack and the Beanstalk*, anyone? So yeah, in the spirit of this section serving as comic relief, let's move right along to the other side of gravitas.

We collectively let this section slide, right, what with its uniformity-defying pair of quotes and all? And you all stop me before I lunge with my outstretched hands for a *third* quote, this one from the lyrics of a song by Elton John—*Hold me closer, tiny dancer*, won't you?

11. Java, Distilled

Who had deceived thee so often as thyself?
- Benjamin Franklin

As you can tell from the pic above—and regular readers know that I've said on several occasions how all pics around here are either mine or culled from the public domain—I like to take notes and highlight. A lot. So it is that, behind the canopy of upright highlighters in the pic, you may, if you peer intently, spy a neat row of books, all cultivated and harvested for your reading pleasure.

In fact, a full *half* of them didn't even make it into this essay. That's selectiveness, all in the quest to serve you the better. Barista, would you please bring us some freshly prepared espressos?

And while we wait to be served, I invite you to linger over the pic above. Soak in the depth-effect. Or something.

12. Bring It In For A Landing

I am very fond of truth, but not at all of martyrdom.
- Voltaire

Wow, the words people will come up with—and get away with—never cease to amaze me. Check that word "unplottable" in the quote above, written with not a little abandon. Sheesh, c'mon. Neologisms notwithstanding, I must confess that the wayward quote, utterly uninformed by the notion of cybernetics and torpedoes, does have a point: Seek, and you shall find.

And so it is that we come full circle. Our well-caffeinated, Java-powered trek—those espressos were good, weren't they?—now draws to a close.

Rubber is about to hit the tarmac. Speaking of which, remember those things we used to board and fly in, around the country, and the world? All that will come back, in good time, especially for you all smitten by wanderlust. But while we stay put nowadays, let's bring this essay in for *its* landing.

Oh yeah, we get to have not one but two quotes. Again.

Life is good.

Let's take it to the limit.

13. A Sturdy Bridge To The Future?

Are we there, yet? Take a deep breath, will you? Why is everyone, like, in such a hurry nowadays?

Whoah. First things first: Like, *how* in the world did this section even make it into this essay? I need to have a chat with my editing staff ("*Shhh... Just between you and me: This is strictly a one-man shop; even calling it a shop borders on the presumptuous. It's all on me. Solo. Uno. I'm writer, editor, designer, publisher, janitor—you name it—around here.*")

But come to think of it, this grand finale of a section isn't such a bad idea after all. In fact, I'm going to call off that chat I was going to have with you-know-who. They've given us the perfect exit, our way to end things with the bang: Building on the metaphor of a bridge—so siphon off all those coffee beans for a moment—Java is uniquely poised to build bridges into the future of production, performant software.

For one thing, the already-thriving ecosystem continues to go places. The Java Virtual Machine (aka *JVM*) is the envy of one and all, deservedly so, being the stellar piece of software machinery that it is, and a mecca for modern languages—Scala and Clojure to name but two—which want to have a piece of the pie, understandably so.

We hardly knew ye, Java.

Craning my neck down a few inches, I noticc a serene, porous, shining-white, bezier-mesh cranium suspended in deep thought, charting unknown vistas—having hopefully loaded enough of a context into its working memory—quite possibly dreaming up the next generation of algorithms, all to be written in... Java?

Only time will tell.

◆ ◆ ◆

CHAPTER 6: MICROSERVICES IN SMALL PIECES

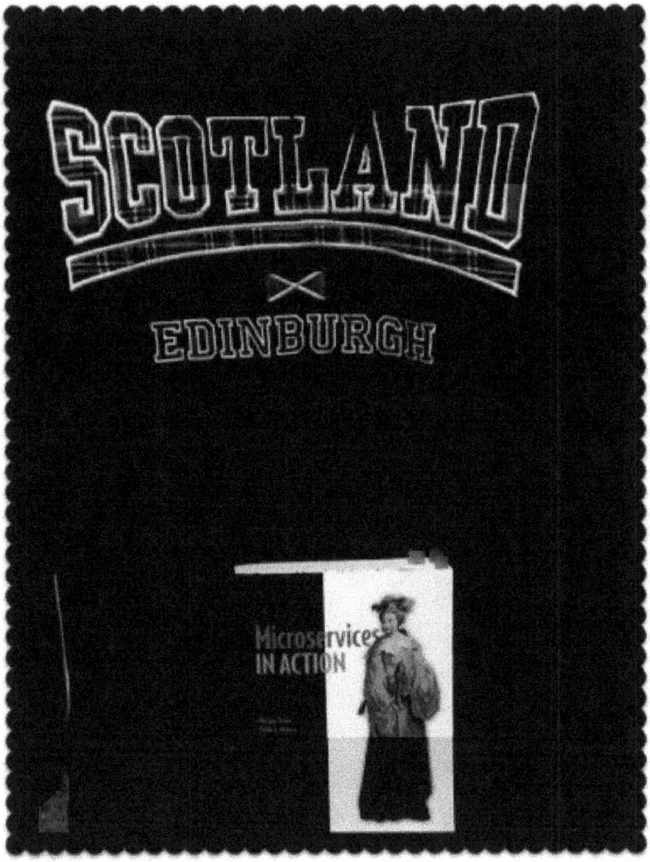

Edinburgh: *(1) The capital city of Scotland , and (2) The name of the latest release of an open-source, microservices-based software project that sprang into life* ***on someone's kitchen island.***

0. Introduction

Before we get ahead of ourselves, let me spill the beans right here....

Here's the deal. We'll be making **a bunch of pit stops** in this essay—a part of which will be to check what's up with each one of the following cool books—as we wend our merry way through the landscape of microservices at large:

1. ***Microservices in Action***, by Morgan Bruce and Paulo Pereira (Manning Publications)
2. ***Microservices Patterns***, by Chris Richardson (Manning Publications)
3. ***The Tao of Microservices***, by Richard Rodger (Manning Publications)
4. ***Building Microservices with Go***, by Nic Jackson (Pakt Publications)
5. ***Building Microservices: Designing Fine-Grained Systems***, by Sam Newman (O'Reilly Media)
6. ***SOA Patterns***, by Arnon Rotem-Gal-Oz (Manning Publications)
7. ***The Model Thinker: What You Need to Know to Make Data Work for You***, by Scott E. Page (Basic Books)
8. ***System Design, Modeling, and Simulation using Ptolemy II***, by Claudius Ptolemaeus, Editor (Dept. of EECS at UC Berkeley)

(Relax, links to *all* eight featured books above appear later in this essay, in their respective entry each.)

Plus **another handful of pit stops**—they will actually appear *before* the book reviews I mention above—are as follows:

- *Yo, Marco Polo!*
- *What's Up With Edinburgh?*
- *Less Is More*
- *So Is More Less?*
- *Perhaps A (Game Of Thrones) Coffee Mug Instead?*
- *Take Two. A Decent Definition of.... Microservices!*
- *But Growth Is Inevitable*
- *We Stood At The Edge, And Wondered...*

If you felt a bit faint on taking in the (motley!) list above, please know—and this point is primarily going to be for our new readers—that we don't (and *won't*) do boring stuff around here. Keeping things light, yet substantive and worth your precious time, remains priority *el numero uno*. My formula is simple: I write what I myself would like to read. Anything less simply doesn't cut it around here.

Yep, that right there is my litmus test. So if (the process of) writing ever begins to feel labored and painful, I know right away that *that's* how it is going to *read*: laborious and pained. On exactly this point, if you ask me, this guy sure knew what he was talking about:

If it sounds like writing, I rewrite it.

~ Elmore Leonard (in *Elmore Leonard's 10 Rules of Writing*)

And yes, *also* appearing in the pic above is my very own sweat-shirt, which I bought last year from a delightful little store (The Pride of Scots) on Princes Street in Edinburgh—I recall a wad of British pounds being exchanged in the transaction—just down from my hotel on Lothian Street where I was staying while attending an EdgeX conference in Edinburgh.

Finally, not to be outdone by the stylists, both of hair and prose—you know the ones who keep yammering about how every essay should have a beginning, a *muddle*, and an end?—we've spun up **an uber-stylish closing section** (and no, not *that* kind of Uber) which will end (possibly upend) this erudite essay, sporting sub-sections such as these:

- *Read My Lips: No Moh' Selfies!*
- *What If We Got Fearful Symmetry?*
- *What If Raindrops Kept Falling On Your Head?*
- *What If The World Suddenly Turned Bokeh, Eh?*
- *Void This Polaroid. Right Now*
- *Doggone It: Daguerreotype Denouement?!*
- *Cookie-cutters, Anyone?*
- *Back-breaking Load Or Something?*
- *Dedication, Plus a Thank You!*

But wait a sec, is that a life-sized statue of famed explorer Marco Polo I see down the street from us? Oh my!

1. Yo, Marco Polo!

"Hey, what's with that Marco Polo statue?", you ask. And glad you did: For one thing, the statue is placed squarely in Ulaanbaatar (Mongolia), which is a hike from Edinburgh (Scotland). For another—and speaking of the renowned traveler Marco Polo—I got a kick out of how one reader recently dubbed me as "the Marco Polo of the programming world".

Well, there sure was no crowning ceremony where you could have seen me kneeling and hearing: "*I hereby dub thee, Sir (Yeah, right!) Akram, as the Marco Polo of the programming world.*" Nope, nothing *half* as fancy as that, which is just as well—you see, I had skinned both my knees from all the traveling I've been doing lately, especially from scuttling around on my knees after lost luggage at airports—because going down on bruised knees can be mighty painful.

But I digress: New(er) readers catching—and latching—on to this "digressions" thing, eh?

2. What's Up With Edinburgh?

And now I get to tell you what's up with Edinburgh, in case its enigmatic mention up atop had made you curious: It simply happens that Edinburgh—in addition of course to being the name of Scotland's lovely capital city—is also the name of the upcoming release of an open-source, microservices-based software project that began life on someone's kitchen island (Emphasis on kitchen is all the more appropriate since we engineers and computer scientists have been known to cook algorithmic recipes, and brew up algorithms and stuff like that.)

Oh, as we get ready to put our understanding of microservices on a solid footing, plus check out some fantastic resources—remember that handful of worthy books on microservices I introduced up atop?—I want you to look out for a *South Korean* mascot to make a guest appearance (or two) further down.

Just saying, because, should you ever grow wistful for all things *Scottish*, I've got you covered there, too! Yep, just check what happened when we decided to mix—after all, we were chatting about cooking up (algorithmic) recipes just a sec ago—yer Edinburgh ode with microservices (Read at your own digestive risk.)

3. Less Is More

See that cluster of cutie mushrooms above, each one pliantly trained in one direction like synchronized radar disks? Does it remind you of organic growth? Well, if ever there were a counterpart to organic growth in the world of software development, it sure would resemble what we know and love today as microservices.

Fair enough, or are you tempted to relegate this to the bin of Harley Davidson motorcycles-inspired wisdom such as

If I tried to explain, you wouldn't understand.

Now ain't that right? Well, for one thing, there is no shame whatsoever in meagerness of size or footprint. Take it from legendary programmer Rob Pike who—in running ever farther than most with the quote above that *Less is more, in prose as in architecture*—transplanted some (bricks-and-mortar) architectural wisdom into some equally wise (bits-and-bytes) architectural wisdom by noting that

Less is exponentially more

If ever you've done a decent bit of programming in the Go programming language as I have—hey, check out my adventures in the land of Go—you'll appreciate what Pike is yammering about.

Flickr is temporarily down for scheduled maintenance
Sad, sad panda wants photos!

4. So, Is More Less?

That is to say, if we agreed earlier that less is more... Hey, let's call it off, and never mind such highfalutin (tautological) skirmishes—let's delegate those to the land of UNIX where we have tools called less and more; no, really, there are tools with exactly those names, and which could only have from the minds of sandal-wearing, bearded, UNIX wizards.

OK, so this is what (really) happened: I decided that I wanted to give you all a break from scaling *yet* another wall of text, lest you tune out; can't have that happen. Hence the bright yellow-bordered postage stamp pic below, yay! (I'm telling you, the attention span of our generation is getting smaller and smaller, even as we speak....)

And what happened next—honest—was that the Flikr site was down. See, um, my *proof of purchase* above about the service outage; I'm tell you, it *did* happen!

DESIGN
HARRY POTTER

5. Perhaps A (Game Of Thrones) Coffee Mug Instead?

Well, given the Flikr site outage, I couldn't really grab a nice pic or two to stick above in order to give you all a break from scaling yet another wall of text. In turn, what you do get today is the bright yellow-bordered postage stamp that was actually meant for a future blog post—essay, really (You've probably gathered by now that an essay is what I like to call one of these critters-that-one-posts-to-blogsites....)

Well, since the cat is now (officially) out of the bag—my having divulged the theme of the next blog post—I invite you to check the analogical reasoning going on in the pic above: A piquant parallelism or two, perhaps related to wizened wizardry, yeah? Most of all, check the *12-pack chewing gum box* I found on our set —man, if only the cleaning crew would be a bit more diligent when they sweep through our staging area!—and which I immediately, and every-so-slyly, quarantined to the confines of the yellow oval, which I trust you *also* see in the pic above.

Hmm... Maybe everything in that jaundiced yellow *does* need to be quarantined away, which is just as well. Anyhow, you probably heard (by now) that the infamous coffee cup in that Game of Thrones episode has now vanished. And a good thing it did; it was getting on my nerves.

For the whole nine yards on the analogical reasoning and blending of paradigms—including of course our very own *12-pack chewing gum box* found smack in the middle of our stage—you'll just have to wait until the next essay. Fair enough?

6. Take Two. A Decent Definition of.... Microservices!

No more spoilers, please; paradigm-blending coolness and parallelism-prettiness will simply have to wait till next time.... For crying out loud, I'm the lone imprimatur around here who toils away at designing, writing, and in general the lovely work of ideation; according to a competing theory, though, all I do around here is "glue and staple."

Regardless, do take some comfort in knowing that all this mishmash will become eventually consistent; as in, try singing Brewer's CAP Theorem to The Rolling Stones' memorable song *You Can't Always Get What You Want.* (More details here, if you want to get what you *need*, amirite?)

Closer at hand, meanwhile, and carrying on with trying to put our understanding of microservices on a stolid—yes, not solid, *stolid*—footing, let's trudge onward.

Goodness, even *more* mushrooms coming up? Darn.

7. But Growth Is Inevitable

That's right, remember those itty-bitty mushrooms we ran into earlier? Well, they grew and grew, all the while remaining faithfully trained in one direction—sunflower-like, though I really have no idea why!—until they became behemoths. And they multiplied.

Then we got ourselves even *more* mushrooms!

But words are things, and a small drop of ink, falling,
like dew, upon a thought;
Produces that which makes thousands, perhaps millions think.

~ Byron

For the final word on (those *once*-itty-bitty!) mushrooms, I invite you to check this marvelously erudite conversation thread that took place in the *Comments* section of our very own blogsite, some moons ago, though.

So it is with the organic growth—pardon the anthropomorphism—that we witness daily in the world of software development. But who is forcing whose hand? (Yo, is that *you*, Adam Smith, with the invisible hand. Hmm... Now there's a connection!) Dunno, really. Sigh. Why don't we let The Bard have a try?

Your gentleness shall force,
More than your force move us to gentleness.

~ William Shakespeare (in *As You Like It*)

That's just a fancy way of saying (every word The Bard uttered was fancy, after all) that we want not to force growth; rather, relentless growth forces itself on *us*. It's inevitable. We're dealing with the most malleable stuff to be found in the industrial world—nope, not talking about mushrooms any more—and which, of course, we all know and love as software. Watch out, software *is* eating the world, after all, in pieces small and big.

So what do we do? Throw our hands up in despair in an angst-ridden fit?

Oh no, we don't! We have our ways; we know how to tackle, repair, and reverse the rot (and in fact *prevent* that rot from taking root in the first place!)

Yes, there *is* a way: it's called *the tao of microservices*. Read on to find out how and why...

You feeling better already? Yeah?

8. We Stood At The Edge, And Wondered...

Why, check out the diaper-clad toddler in the pic above, squarely facing that algae-clad thingamajig ahead in deep meditation: Isn't that a flashback to our own childhood, strolling and playing, with a PeePal or two, on the shores of pBay.

But then we came across this Big Ball of Mud or something? Darn, someone should have warned us back then, us then-toddlers with a simpler, more-direct message such as: Here be dragons, or something.

I ain't going in there for sure, no more! (Who knows *how* many millions of penicillin molds fester in that grotesque ball of mud?!) Got enough troubles on my hand as is, without inviting a boatload of germs from that infernal infestation on the sandy shore, you know ;)

But a fine pasture for scientific investigation that sure would've made for Pasteur (the French chemist and microbiologist of yesteryear) who made a name for himself by, among other things, noting that "*Chance only favors the prepared mind.*"

But I digress, and grow weary, as in

But, hey, I got good news for all of us: Yay, it's finally time to dive headlong into our survey of the tools—it's books all the way down, I'm telling you—and which we need to slice our way through a Ball of Mud, or two, or three...

Yep, the time has come for us to make a bunch of pit stops—checking out some microservices wisdom and tools by way of a handful of worthy books—as wend our merry way through the landscape of microservices at large.

SCOTLAND
Microservices
IN ACTION

9. #1 Microservices in Action, by Morgan Bruce and Paulo Pereira (Manning Publications)

- Overall excellent book, with a pragmatic outlook (all stuff, no fluff, high SNR)
- Just don't expect—if you judged so from the elegant cover—any sort of Elizabethan finery over teacups, with gentle piano-playing in the background.) Nope, it's all about what goes on (or at least, what *should* go on!) in the trenches of developing microservices in the wild.
- Profusely illustrated with helpful diagrams (The folks at Manning sure got their formula right!)

10. #2 Microservices Patterns, by Chris Richardson (Manning Publications)

- You're going to find a ton of distilled industry wisdom between the covers of this fine book.
- Yes, the examples are all in Java, but many (if not all!) ideas are eminently portable to other programming languages. So even if you develop microservices in another language—I've been doing exactly that for a year now in the Go programming language—you'll gain quite a bit from this book.
- Wait a second, what's that Korean doll doing in the pic above? The people in Korea are so nice and gracious; I was there recently and can attest to that! The Korean language remains foreign to me...
- ...but judging from the grunts coming from the Korean doll (in the stuffy box in which it finds itself encased), it appears to be intoning: "*Hey, it's stuffy in here. I can barely breathe... Somebody get me out! That 12 hour (non-stop) flight from Seoul to San Francisco was long enough, what with having to be stuck in a cardboard box, for crying out loud!*")
- Whoah! Help is on the way (see the pic coming up next), both for our Korean doll *and* for all of us looking for even more generous servings of microservices wisdom.

SCOTLAND

11. #3 The Tao of Microservices, by Richard Rodger (Manning Publications)

- Should you decide—trust me, we *all* have budgets!—to get yourself only one book from this list, make it this one. You won't go wrong.
- This book is incredible: While you won't find much code in its pages, the book is replete with rock-solid advice on getting a grip on harnessing microservices.
- Many books have a tendency to gloss over the hard stuff; hey, as an author, *I'll* unabashedly fess up and profess that I've done (more than) my own share of handwaving.
- But not this one; the author has a remarkably subtle —and endearingly charming—sense of humor, which shines through the pages.
- Be sure to not miss the plethora of footnotes (Frankly, there's more wisdom in some of them than can be found in whole chapters of other books!)
- Whoah! "*Finally,*" says our Korean doll, "*somebody came to my rescue, and not a moment too soon!*"
- So there you have it, our Korean pal is finally unfettered and free, breathing the fresh Austin air (after the near-suffocating trauma of traveling in a cardboard box for multiple hours.)
- Hey, good things take a long time, don't they say? Meanwhile, check out our pal's fancy clothes—Oh my! It's getting ready to do some fancy footwork... It can do karate. Chop, chop, ninja! Take that, now...
- Things getting dangerous in this neighborhood... Getting out of here. *Quick!*

SCOTLAND
EDINBURGH
Building
Microservices
with Go

12. #4 Building Microservices with Go, by Nic Jackson (Pakt Publications)

- Like Winston Churchill said—and I'm quoting from memory as I don't particularly feel like looking up references at the moment—on one gloomy day, many moons ago, "*Give us the tools, man, and we'll get the job done.*"
- OK, OK, I get it; different times, different settings. Sheesh, some people got no sense of humor! Anyhow, and come to think of it, we software types work in the trenches, too, don't we?
- Ah yes, and to get our job done—and remember what I said earlier about the polyglot nature of our industry?—we need hands-on stuff. And this book delivers in spades
- See all those tape flags sticking out from my well-worn copy of this book (in the pic above)? This one is a keeper.
- But first, please send in Detective Tintin, will you please? (Watch out, Tintin, please don't trip on those jagged tape flags sticking out from the book, especially now that you've made it safely back with me all the way from Edinburgh!) We have a stormy mystery brewing on our hands...
- Keep reading to find what's up with that.

SCOTLAND
Building Microservices

13. #5 Building Microservices, by Sam Newman (O'Reilly Media)

- So who is going to solve the baffling mystery—no, not the birds and the bees—of how bees manage to distill honey?
- But Akram, what's this *beekeeping* thing got to do with microservices, for crying out loud?
- "*Patience, and you'll learn a lot!*", I reply sanguinely. OK, so while you won't find any beekeeping advice in this book, it has generous servings of distilled—see, right there is our running metaphor of distillation—wisdom on wherewithal of microservices, served up honeycomb-style.
- Seriously, though, this one is another keeper: all stuff, no fluff
- It also happens to be the very first book through which I taught myself the ins and outs of what's so special about microservices.
- Wow, did anyone even notice that curvy, S-shaped, pliable ruler in the pic above, striking an elegant pose as if it were born for showtime? My late father (a chemical engineer by profession) got that blue ruler for when I was in high school so I could draw curved graphs.
- Life moves on. Don't move on before checking this book out...

SCOTLAND
EDINBURGH
MARINE
AQUARIUM
SOA
PATTERNS

14. #6 SOA Patterns, by Arnon Rotem-Gal-Oz (Manning Publications)

- So there you have. Even if you didn't take my word for it earlier—I'm merely the messenger, you know—I hope the excerpt above helps you understand the lineage of what we nowadays know and love as microservices.
- Oh, speaking of designing data-intensive applications, should you wish to delve into Kafkaesque stuff—as in *Apache* Kafka plus a hefty dollop of *Franz* Kafka-style metaphysics thrown in for good measure—we got you covered there, too: Check what happened when some of us got Krazy About Kafka!
- This is a richly-illustrated and well-done book—as in neither under-done nor over-done!—that's going to be well worth your time.
- Wouldn't you agree at this time that the *only* thing fishy thing remaining is that marine aquarium screen-saver box—yes folks, there *was* a time when CDs roamed the earth!—which you see in the pic above? ��
- OK, good. So let's call off our emergency page to Detective Tintin; my brother is a cardiologist, so I know (*second*-hand anyway) a thing or two about getting paged.

SCOTLAND
EDINBURGH
SCOTT E. PAGE
THE MODEL THINKER

15. #7 The Model Thinker, by Scott E. Page (Basic Books)

- What, for crying out loud, we had finished calling off our emergency page to Detective Tintin. Yet he swaggers in now, feigning bluster, and his mouth agape in amazed disbelief? C'mon, know it off, Tintin; we see through your act, latecomer! *Wow*, with (so-called!) trusty friends like that, we're going to need Scotland Yard's number programmed on speed-dial.
- Speaking of which... Hmm... I wonder if that bright-red, quintessentially-British telephone booth in the pic still works; if it does, that's what we use for programming our speed-dial! Yay, we got it.
- Meanwhile, why don't you take in the happenings in the pic above? Now is that the beatific scene of the paragon of modeling or what?
- "*Yo, what's modeling got to do with microservices?*," you ask blithely.
- Hmm... Might need to page the book's author, Scott E. Page—or should it be *Scotty* from the esteemed USS Enterprise of Star Trek fame?—to beam us up, if you know what I'm saying?
- Odd, I see someone's (eminently non-business-looking!) business card tucked into the top of Scott E. Page's fine book. "*Like, what's up with that?*" Whoah, wait, one thing at a time, dude!
- But first, a word on modeling... "*Uh oh, here Akram goes digressing.*"
- But seriously, check this brilliant formulation by Stuart Russell in his Foreword to the fine book *Practical Probabilistic Programming* by Avi Pfeffer (Manning Publications) as he goes down memory lane, talking about how,

- So there you have it. And even if you didn't take my word for it earlier—do you, ever?—I hope the excerpt above helps you get a sense for the noble lineage of modeling. It's totally slick. Plus it's trending, and in style, I'm telling you; math *never* goes out of style.
- Yeah, but why should you listen to moi? Well, for starters, I invite you to check out my thoughts on modeling as done in the context of *deep learning*.
- When you visit the aforesaid link, be sure to check out the evergreen quote by George Box ("*Essentially, all models are wrong, but some are useful*".) Gotta appreciate that guy's sense of clarity, amirite?
- Model first, then design, and then—and *only* then—develop your software; you'll sleep better at night. Just sayin'.
- Moving on to our final (book) entrant in the field....

16. #8 System Design, Modeling, and Simulation using Ptolemy II (EECS @ UC Berkeley)

- You're no doubt muttering with hushed words, "*Goodness, Akram is serious about this modeling business, darn!*" Well, just when when thought it was safe to continue reading—after all, I had dispensed with some metaphysics such as how math *never* goes out of style—here I am again, eager to pick up even *more* finer points of modeling.

Explaining Metaphysics to the nation–
I wish he would explain his Explanation
~ Lord Byron (from *Don Juan: Dedication*)

- Seriously, though, this is an idea-dense book; pretty high SNR, if you ask me.
- And if you dig *system* thinking, you're going to love this thick, juicy book—it weighs in at just over 700 pages (Hey, I just confirmed that number—for all you doubters out there, lol—only after reaching into the bookshelf and pulling out my copy, given to me as a gift by Edward Ashford Lee while on the UC Berkeley campus a couple of years ago when he pulled his personal copy out of *his* bookshelf (he's the Robert S. Pepper Distinguished Professor Emeritus in the EECS Department at Berkeley.)
- The demo he gave me (of the reference implementation, *Ptolemy II*) was pretty cool, too. But I digress.
- The point is is this: The essential engineer not only chisels with a mind informed by mathematical precision, he also *draws* with the hands imbued by the passion of an artist (And here I invite you to check the Escher-style, framed drawing in the pic above, also courtesy of Edward.)

- Speaking of this blending of engineering and art, I can scarcely do better than point you in the direction of a handful of resources:
  1. *Plato And The Nerd*
  2. *Return of Plato And The Nerd*
  3. *Plato And The Nerd Strikes Back*
- Enough reading material (for *now*, anyway)?
- Should you wish to delve deeper still into modeling goodness (with *Ptolemy II*), though, I invite you to check out a reasonably in-depth write-up under the guise of: *Software Actors, Rare Benefactors*.

17. Read My Lips: No Moh' Selfies!

Wait, wait, wait... *Honest*, this time. Or has your traumatized memory—well, I confess it hasn't been *that* long since we peered into the soul of edge computing, refracted as it was through a dozen selfies—ushered in a cavalry of ghosts? Yo, Casper ;)

Look at it this way: The work of design invariably involves peering deep into abstract stuff, amirite or what? So what's wrong with some self-reflection, eh? And frankly, all I'm doing (in the pic above, anyway) is emerging from a daylong planning and design session not so long ago...

And since we happened to be talking compassion—I mean *selfie*—fatigue, let's put things in perspective. Trust me, and this is especially for those moaning and groaning about my pics, you'll be counting your blessings in five seconds flat! Check this...

18. What If We Got Fearful Symmetry?

Tyger Tyger, burning bright,
In the forests of the night;
What immortal hand or eye,
Could frame thy fearful symmetry?

~ William Blake (in ***The Tyger***)

Man, those poets need to get their spellings right ("*Tyger*", for example: Sheesh, for crying out loud!) I mean, I feel like wielding some poetic license and refactoring—um, I mean, rewording—the poem by, for starters, renaming it The "*Tigger*" right now.

(Hint: Count your blessings, because I could have regaled you with... *The Tigger*)

19. What If Raindrops Kept Falling On Your Head?

I'm soaking wet! Such bountiful rain... "*Hey,*" asks this bedraggled blogger, "*are we in Seattle or something?*"

(Reminder: Count your blessings, because we *could* have been. You know what I'm saying?)

20. What If The World Suddenly Turned Bokeh, Eh?

Atomic: *In the context of concurrent operations, it describes an operation which appears to take effect at a single point in time so that another concurrent process can't encounter the operation in a "half-finished" state.*

Ah, atoms, atoms, everywhere? *Especially* those bokeh atoms adorning our hapless, symmetry-defying microservices book in the pic above: My bad, and a rookie mistake to smudge the pic with a smidgen of bokeh. Darn. But look, it'll all *eventually* become consistent... in the cosmic reality of things, in the grand scheme of things.

(Subtle hint: Please, I *implore* you, count your blessings, because, solar flares notwithstanding, we could be bombarded with a barrage of bokeh atoms, willy nilly, as in that Indiana Jones movie where he goes tumbling down the street in a fridge!)

21. Void This Polaroid. Right Now

Wait, what *kind* of snapshot are we talking about anyway, the Polaroid kind or the DDD one?!

(Gentle reminder: Count your blessings, *please*, because, instead of the primrose-pretty and popular alternative to traditional snapshot-only persistence that is event sourcing, we could instead have been talking about grungy old snapshot isolation and repeatable reads! And yes, you could be forgiven for thinking that it does everything that a transaction needs to do. But let's eject from purgatory *and* similar contemplations, such as our ill-starred hero Peyton Farquhar in Ambrose Bierce's *An Occurrence at Owl Creek Bridge*. Brr... Shiver-me-timbers, as our spunky, spinach-munching Popeye would say.)

22. Doggone It: Daguerreotype Denouement?!

Jack London wrote this book called Martin Eden—and which I had to study as an undergrad—from which we learned about this thing called a denouement! It's like the unraveling of a ritornello or something.

(Penultimate hint: Do count your blessings, won't you? Or would you rather try to unravel the complex layers of an autodidact's unrequited love writ large across the pages of Jack London's aforementioned book? Just sayin'.)

23. Cookie-cutters, Anyone?

We could slice and dice—cookie-cutter-style—*every* which way around the software design landscape! And all we get out of that was the neon-bordered postage stamp (above) with yet another facet of fearful symmetry writ upon it? Darn.

(Final squabble: But hey, *this* may be something we technology types can dig. You know, stuff such as carving design out of nothing at all as we go about realizing designs in code. And symmetry has shone the brightest (in the land of code anyway) with the light of Lisp—with its uniquely unmatched notion of homoiconicity, where code is data and data is code—specifically the Lisp dialect with which I'm familiar: Clojure.)

24. Back-breaking Load Or Something?

So heavy was the load that we had to call in the troops (above) from the martial arts academy! As in corporeal matters, so in matters of bits and bytes. But I'm sure you—and *I* certainly do—want to keep things lean when it comes to software.

Yep, best to keep software lean. Let microservices be your allies in this endeavor. Cool? Until next time, then? No? You want *more?!*

Ah, you see—sharp reader that you are—I realize that I owe you a *Dedication*. Do this: Walk the primrose path (right around the chocolate red rose), and you'll find what you're looking for. Promise.

25. Dedication, Plus a Thank You!

Last, but certainly not least, here is the *Dedication* I had hinted at: That gorgeous rose is for my sweetheart—my wife—who helps me stay grounded (on earth) so that, with both feet firmly planted on the ground, I can keep reaching for the stars.

And a big thank you to my dear readers (*just* like you!) who keep me motivated with comments such as these:

- I wonder, "Where in the world did he get the time, energy, and brain power to construct such an essay?"
- You definitely put a brand new spin on...
- Welcome back, Marco Polo of the programming world!
- You are so cool!
- Rarely do I come across a blog that's...
- You make blogging look easy.
- It's always nice to see your wonderful brain at work, Sir Akram!
- You ought to take part in a contest for one of the best sites on the web!
- Hi! I like your writing so so much!
- Great post Akram.
- Build things with care.
- Another excellent post Akram.
- Hey Akram. Great essay as usual...
- Your passion and dedication towards writing clearly shows...
- Fascinating essay!
- Great essay Akram, the new formatting is much better now
- Goodness Akram! You've actually managed to out do yourself by a factor of 41!
- Hi Akram, I think a lot of us were introduced to the

wave/particle-like duality of OO/FP by Scala...

- Well done, Sir Akram!
- Truly enlightening for a budding (wannabe) Computer Scientist like me.
- It's Amazing! Am exceptionally glad to peruse your blog.
- This blog awesome and i learn a lot about programming from here

(**Life Vest-style Warning:** Some of the links above will take you to our old blog site—which I no longer maintain and where the visitor count was 111,208 last time I checked and which has tonnes of comments—so do be sure to navigate *right* back to this, our new blog site. Please don't be left stranded in the twilight zone; I promise to set up a redirect to automate that, but don't hold your breath for that.)

And with that, we draw this essay to a close—for real this time. Until next time, then.

As for anyone so bold as to operate along the dictums of a certain *Rolling Stones* song (*I Can't Get No Satisfaction*), and you really, *really* must know where the inspiration for the title of this essay—***M****icroservices* ***In*** ***S****mall* ***P****ieces*—came from, we've got you covered, too: So I was inspired by the acrostic title of Christian Queinnec's hard-hitting tome on ***LISP*** named ***L****isp* ***In*** ***S****mall* ***P****ieces* (Cambridge University Press, 2003). Ah, Lisp; so sweet, so tantalizing. For more of my thoughts on that language, which is the *LISP* dialect (Clojure) that runs flawlessly on the JVM, and one in which, sadly, I hardly do any programming any more, you can find the whole stash here.

◆ ◆ ◆

CHAPTER 7: THE 3 SECRETS OF WINNING WILLPOWER

0. Intro

Obstacles are those frightful things you see when you take your eyes off your goal.
~ Henry Ford

What? A Multiple-choice Question!

What was the first thought that crossed your mind when you saw those two words—"Winning Willpower"—appear together in the title above? Choose from the following three choices:

- **A.** Willpower that sets you on a winning streak?
- **B.** The act itself of wooing—hence, *winning*—willpower so as to make it yours?
- **C.** Winsome willpower, if there can be such a thing?

If you answered with an "*All of the above*", you're super-close, because the correct answer is: "*Choices **A** and **B***" (Choice **C** borders, dare I say, on the metaphysical, so we'll skip that for now.) And if you ran away, stricken with test-taking fright, please come right back; you have my solemn pledge that not another multiple-choice question will rear its head from here onward.

All I was doing there was setting the stage. And how better to do that than by helping you connect this willpower business with some related, recent musings. Enter creativity, which, as you may recall, had been on our minds lately: We had dissected the ins and outs of creativity like never before, amirite?

Something Had Been Missing

Then I got to thinking that a crucial element had gone missing from our vivisections. On tuning my radar, it dawned on me that I had lapsed, ending up putting the cart before the proverbial horse.

You see, creativity isn't something that *happens* to you; it is something that you *make* happen. "*And exactly how do you do that, Mr. Smartypants Blogger?*", you delicately ask. Glad you did.

Enter willpower.

This time—following on the heels of a handful of deep dives into fathoming the essence of creativity—we explore the groundwork that has to be laid before the chariot of creativity to go trundling forth (and for our creativity chariot to get anywhere, really.) So yeah, having held forth on all things creativity, we rush to make up for our lapse, putting the horse before the proverbial cart.

This Critter Called Willpower

You see, without a critical mass of this critter called willpower, you and I are not going to get anywhere with creativity (*and* with a boatload of other things, for that matter.) Luckily, the horse hasn't left the barn, so let's get right down to business.

(*"Hey Akram, who is that guy with the red woolen cap in the pic above, standing atop what appears to be a peak in a mountain range, his ebullience on conquering the heights on full display?"*, you ask. Well, um, I don't know. What don't *you* take a peek yourself? So there. Hah. I'm getting good at this delegating business.)

Next thing I know, you'll be asking me to find that mountain's grade! Speaking of grades, and albeit of a different flavor, that guy with the red woolen cap gets an **A** grade for social distancing in these times of COVID-19 (especially as there's not another soul in sight.)

1. The Vista Opening Before Us

Fired at first sight with what the Muse imparts,
In fearless youth we tempt the heights of Arts;
~ Alexander Pope

Row, Row, Row Your Boats

The lads on the rowing team above sure are heaving those oars mightily in their fearless youth, aren't they? True grit on display.

I invite you to linger over the scene and see how many metaphors you can glean from the action taking place—In particular, try bringing to mind how our perception itself evolves as we experience life more fully, and how this metaphor (of evolving perception) is expressed elegantly by the sentiment that

> *Beauty is truth's smile when she beholds her own face in a perfect mirror.*
> *- Rabindranath Tagore*

With that sentiment in mind—and its import hopefully impressed on your heart—the vista opening before us has three doors, each of which leads onto a tantalizing terrace of enlightenment:

1. **Remember To Not Get Fooled By Your Body's Reward System**
2. **Get Better At Managing Your Body Budget**
3. **Align Your Work With Your Interests**

One door at a time, we will, together, enter the realm of action taking place therein. We will linger only so long as to pluck the gist of what's happening, with a view to having it help us understand this critter called willpower.

And Keep Rowing

Lads, as you tempt the heights of the Arts, you keep heaving those oars, chopping out water by the bucketful while we revel in the splendor of water suspended in the skies—see those puffy clouds forming the backdrop of the picture coming into view? —a little startled by the amorphousness of the molecules of life.

Let's see if we can begin to see things as *they* are, and perhaps not as *we* are.

Hmm... This is getting a little meta. We had better ground ourselves and get concrete, and dive into it—not the concrete, as that would be mighty painful—divulging one secret at a time. So here we go.

Pronto.

2. Secret #1: Don't Get Fooled By Your Brain's Reward System

The intelligent desire self-control; children want candy.
~ Rumi

Sucked Into The Vortex Of Distraction, Unbidden

It starts innocently enough. With some free time on your hands, you decide to catch up on what's happening in the world of sports, news, books (insert your favorite pursuit here) and find yourself—an hour later—still burrowing unbidden, going deeper and deeper down the rabbit hole.

What just happened there? Well, that's your brain's reward system at work. You see, our brains have evolved to ensure our relentless pursuit of the *promise* of happiness instead of the *experience* of happiness. This is the brain's way of keeping us—much as it did for our ancestors in a different and wilder setting—hunting, gathering, working, and whatnot.

Your Brain's Reward System

And that, ladies and gentlemen, is your brain's reward system, alive and kicking. More details, a *whole* lot more details, can be found in a fine book—one that I highly recommend—entitled *The Willpower Instinct: How Self-Control Works, Why It Matters, and What You Can Do to Get More of It* (Penguin Publishing Group). It's by Kelly McGonigal PhD, who is an award-winning psychology instructor at Stanford University, and a lecturer and program developer at the Stanford Center for Compassion and Altruism Research and Education.

It is not pleasure that makes life worth living. It is life that makes pleasure worth having.
~ George Bernard Shaw

You will find in the pages of *The Willpower Instinct* the lowdown on why we're driven by the *pursuit* of pleasure, but often at the cost of our well-being. It presents in an engaging way the fruits borne after years (think *decades*) of hard science, all carried out by people much smarter than you and I. So yeah, a special area of the brain—the reward center—lights up when it senses pleasurable things coming its way.

And to really, really educate yourself—remember how to be forewarned is to be forearmed—I suggest that you search your digital edition (of *The Willpower Instinct*) by the keywords "reward center" and see for yourself the search results light up your e-reader like a carnival at night, amirite?

Something Pulling Your Strings?

Have you ever pondered on what is perhaps the blight of our lives? Specifically, if you have wondered what our cell phones, the Internet, and other social media may have to do with exploiting our brain's reward system, then this is your book. And if you sensed your reward system light up at the prospects of getting a hold of a new book—*mine* would, the incorrigible sucker for books that I am—then know, too, that this one will reward you many times over.

If you're having challenges with an, um, *surplus* of books in your home (as might be the case in certain other homes down the street), then what I'm going to say next should *not* be held against me. But I'm going to say it anyway: This book is a keeper. Go grab a copy. Rigorous, yet readable. Educational, yet entertaining (when was the last time *that* happened?)

Incidentally, the Rumi quote appearing above also make an appearance—a prominent one—in *The Willpower Instinct, appearing* right after the dedication page.

With our fire lit, we say in synchrony: "*Onward.*"

3. Secret #2: Get Better At Managing Your Body Budget

The desire to seem clever often keeps us from being so.
- Francois de La Rochefoucauld

A Monetary Fable

A disclaimer is in order, especially if you were intrigued by the stash of dough above: I've never seen so many Benjamin Franklins in my life. Truth be told, I've never seen Benjamin *Franklin* in my life. Ever. Only the likes of his appearance—remember the polymath extraordinaire from history books, the one who was a writer, printer, political philosopher, politician, postmaster, scientist, inventor, humorist, civic activist, statesman, and also a diplomat in his spare time?—fittingly commemorated on the face of a certain currency.

I found the picture above in the public domain. (And yes, much like you, I don't have a clue why anyone would spend their precious time taking such outlandish, though evocative, pics.) Oh well, it—awash as it is in tons of a certain denomination—appears here purely to make a point.

And that point is this: My budget is *far* more modest than you may have been led to believe after glancing at the gazillion Benjamin Franklin denomination huddled together—more like stacked up—in their two-dimensional existence, and getting an **F** grade in the process for observing social distancing rather poorly in these COVID-19 days. (Think, if you will, though unromantically enough, to the novella *Flatland: A Romance of Many Dimensions* if the dimensional allusion strike you as a bit disorienting or, frankly, as quirky.)

Heh, the point I *am* trying to make is that you and I each also have a non-monetary budget, one that impacts us in far more immediate ways than our monetary one. And what might that influential budget look like?

Well, welcome to your body's very own budget.

Hello, Body Budget!

One more time, the budget I have in mind for you has nothing whatsoever to do with that *fiscal* stuff; I'm talking about the *physical* stuff, the stuff of our very flesh and bones. Hmm... I see your brows starting to furrow in knots of protestations at such an assertion. Trust me, I'm not making this one up: Your body really *does* have a budget.

And the last word on the subject—that of your body budget—can be found between the two covers of a fine book entitled *How Emotions Are Made: The Secret Life of the Brain* (Mariner Books). It's by Lisa Feldman Barrett PhD, who is a University Distinguished Professor of Psychology at Northeastern University, with appointments at Harvard Medical School and Massachusetts General Hospital in Psychiatry and Radiology.

Starting with an engaging primer on what this body budget business is all about—how your brain budgets the energy in your body to safeguard your wellbeing—the author does a masterful job of making the case for acquiring a better understanding of your predictive brain in conjunction with your body budget. (Those who either deal or dabble with predictive analytics will get a kick out it. *I* sure did.)

Like Sand Through The Hourglass

Like the cycles of the ocean, with tides ebbing and then receding, your body budgeting has its own circadian rhythms, automatically sending you signals to, for example, *replenish* your body's energy by eating, drinking, and sleeping. Conversely, you *spend* energy by engaging in various activities

And this is where the brain's amazing predictive capabilities kick into high gear. At least they should. Guess what? You get to have a say in how you manage all of this spending and replenishing, taking your brain's constant predictions (about your body's energy requirements) as best as you can.

You guessed it. Yep, *this* is where you come in and make a difference: use your brain's (predictive) signals wisely and reap the rewards of a smoothly running operation that is your body, in concert, of course, with everything that makes us human —our emotions, feelings, perception, attentiveness, consciousness, and so forth.

Remember that recharging the expending the body budget go hand-in-hand.

What Will You Do?

The better you get at managing your body budget, the more you harness willpower, which (i.e. willpower) has been scientifically shown to become more manageable when your body budget is being handled—by you, of course—in increasingly intelligent ways.

So go forth and flourish, using your newly acquired knowhow as a guide to conquering willpower.

Let me say it one more time: I wasn't making this one up. Your body *does* have a budget. Tend to it intelligently, and you'll reap the rewards. I'm working on it myself—my energy budget, that is, and definitely not the part having to do with confabulating or speaking in parables (or dabbling with investing a certain currency, for that matter.)

Enough said.

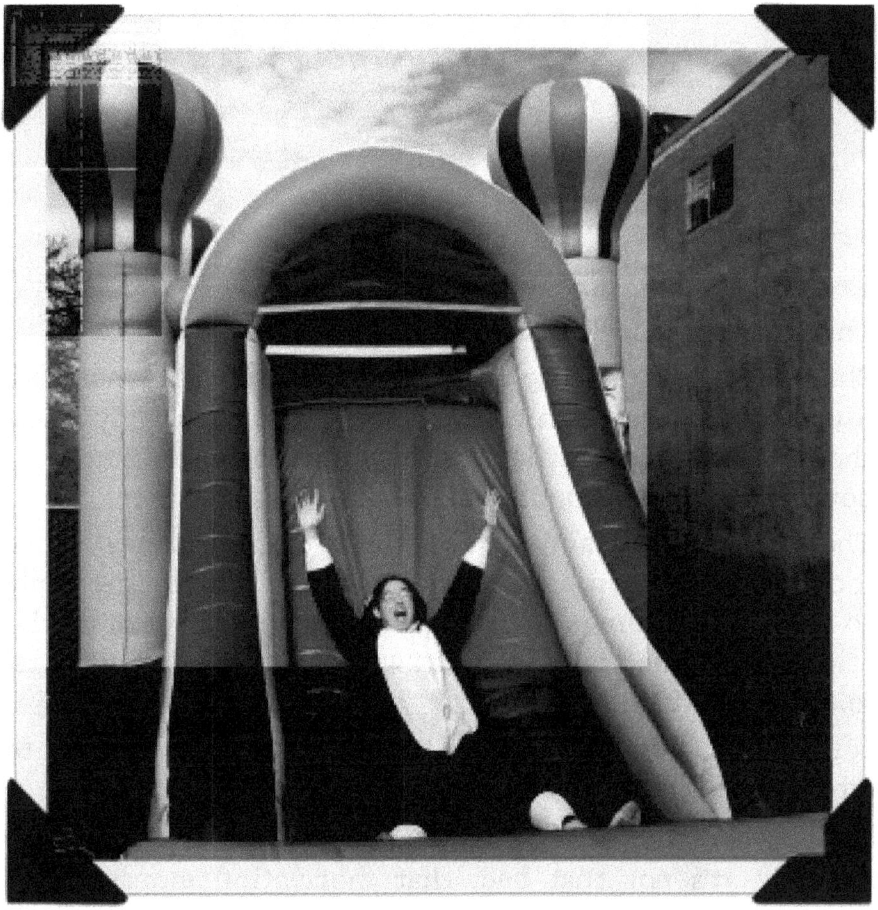

4. Secret #3: Align Your Work With Your Interests

Choose a job you love, and you will never have to work a day in your life.
~ Confucius

Yay, This Is Fun!

That inflatable slide sure looks like a lot of fun.

Plus it leads us directly to encapsulating Secret #3 in a nutshell: If you choose a job that brings you joy, you effectively lower the barriers to entry in the realm of your motivation. Your willpower, in turn, gets a boost and things follow from there.

The basic idea here is one of *lowering* the barriers to entry when it comes to human motivation. Of course, if that doesn't apply to you—if boredom is alien to you and your engines of motivation are automatically revving 24x7—then you deserve to rejoice in the happenstance!

For the *rest* of us, we don't get to have it that easy; we get to wrestle with the motivation monster.

The Right Chemistry

Actually, it's not that bad, that motivation monster; just grumpy at times. Seriously, though—and I first came across this idea in the pages of Shawn Achor's *The Happiness Advantage: The Seven Principles of Positive Psychology that Fuel Success and Performance at Work*—you can make your life easier by aligning your work with your interests more and more. If you are lucky, there will come a day in life when you find yourself reveling in the quote above from Confucius ("*Choose a job you love, and you will never have to work a day in your life.*")

It's easier said that done. But it *can* be done.

And here I would be remiss if I didn't remind you—and myself even more so—that it's far easier *said* than done. Sigh, a whole lot more has usually been *said* than done after everything's been said and done.

But I digress.

And Your Point Is?

The point is: You can, given enough gumption, eventually find resonance with your work—work that you've of course been aligning with what lights your fire and floats your boat—at which time it ceases to be "work"; it gives you joy. You find yourself in a state of "flow."

Ask any virtuoso and she or he will confirm that time flies when they're engaged in their life's work. (The phrase "being in the zone" is likely to come up.)

One genius in particular, perhaps the *prototypical* genius—if there be such a critter—opined poignantly that

Men of lofty genius, when they are doing the least work, are most active.

~ Leonardo da Vinci

(A tad recursive—a genius speaking *of* genius. Oh well; all in a day's work.)

Remember, the more you align your work with your interests, the more you boost your willpower—*jujitsu*-style, by lowering the barriers to entry in the realm of motivation. If you choose a job you resonate with, then you choose to have fun doing what you love, as presaged by Confucius.

One More Time Please

And if I haven't driven you crazy yet—my friends and fans love me all the same—let's call this a wrap. But *not* before some final words of gravitas, words that just might rock you with the force of a sawmill.

Ready for some buzz?

5. Wrap Up

Start Me Up

Speaking of standing up—and I hope you got a kick like I did out of the wry humor standing starkly in the quote above—I invite you to stay tuned for a final announcement which will be made at the end.

Meanwhile, let me remind us all that what one fool can do, another can, too. Together, we've hewn thorough a pile of material and sawed through a boatload of timber. Well, at least the guy standing up in the pic above did. All good, except... "*Cough, cough, what's with all those noxious-looking fumes in the background? No environmental protection, for crying out loud? No nothing?*"

But there you have it, a log enters on one end of the sawmill and lumber exits on the other. Can we build it? "*Yes we can!*"

But I digress.

Where We Went

To recap—appropriately enough, as we call it a wrap—today we explored willpower from three vantage points:

1. **Remember To Not Get Fooled By Your Body's Reward System**
2. **Get Better At Managing Your Body Budget**
3. **Align Your Work With Your Interests**

I invite you to revisit each one of the three—now or later—and let the ideas soak in. I know I'll be doing exactly that: I write as much for you as I do for myself, reminding you that success is decidedly (pun not intended) not a zero-sum game.

A Celebration In The Making

Meanwhile, remember the guy you and I met at the beginning, the one wearing that red woolen cap, standing atop a mountain peak, celebrating his conquest with an almighty lunge? Well guess what. He's still there, and he's *still* lunging. Darn. Some people get carried away, amirite?

But if you and I manage to conquer willpower, either by ourselves or in our togetherness—details to follow, so stay tuned—I'll be the first one to cheer you on (and I know you'll do the same for me) in a celebration worth a mountain of gold.

Treasures untold await you: What are you waiting for?

Let your future unfold.

Stop reading—you can always linger here plus return and read to your heart's content—and get going.

Now.

◆ ◆ ◆

CHAPTER 8: DOMAIN-DRIVEN DESIGN (DDD) DEFIES DOGMA

0. Prelude

See that Tower of Babel in the picture above? Okay, so the Babel Fish was one thing—especially for you all fans of Douglas Adams' book The Hitchhikers Guide To The Galaxy—and the Tower of Babel quite another, with the latter being the one we're talking about here (Let me guess: The first thing that came to your mind at the mention of the Tower of Babel was the clamor arising from throngs of people in a collective din, clamoring past one other as they all speak in their own distinct languages, past others' monologues in their languages!)

But before we get sucked into the Babel vortex—look, it could have been a whole different
vortex that we as a society could've gotten pulled into (actually, already *is*, the inexorable digital vortex, that is)—let's all of us take a big, deep breath.

1. Dedication

My regular readers are of course well aware that it's only the rarest of occasion and time when I dedicate an essay or two to an individual; this is such an occasion, and this is such a time.

With that, I dedicate this essay to Githesh Ramamurthy who is one of the clearest-eyed leaders, embodying what it means to lead by example: He leads with integrity, intelligence, wit, passion, and grace. Githesh is a mentor, benefactor, and friend.

Whenever you read these words—and I know that you've always carved time out of your super-busy schedule to read what I offer on this blog—please know that your encouragement, plus the priceless lessons that I've learned from you, Githesh, will serve me well for a lifetime, especially so at this juncture as I prepare for the quest to help change the world of the Internet of Things (IoT) as we know it today!

2. Preamble (By Way Of A Dialogue)

—Reader: Hey Akram, so whatever this DDD (Domain-Driven Design) thing is anyway, we're willing to give it a listen. But what—more properly, "who"—in the world is this "Dogma" that you mention in the same breath as the title of this essay: "Domain-Driven Design (DDD) Defies Dogma"?

—**Akram:** Um, so the "Dogma" part of the story goes something like this: Being the inveterate cat-lover that you all know me as, I nevertheless once took pity on and gave shelter to a dog whose Ma was somewhat indisposed. So this dog's Ma, as I was saying...

—**Reader:** Yo, stop. Stop *right* there! Heaven help us, Akram, lest you take it upon yourself to start spinning yarns *again*. (Dude, we are *still* licking our wounds after being exposed to your balderdash—that wasn't so long ago either—having to do with your recursive take on *Reveling In The Glory Of Software (On A Stormy Night!)*)

—**Akram:** May I inform your gentle ears that the name—*Programming Digressions* but of course—of our blog site may have something to do with digressing. But hey, we will digress no more! Instead, we'll dive headfirst into the coolness of DDD. Cool?

—**Reader:** We'll believe that when we *see* it. But yeah, go ahead...

3. Outside, Looking In

Would you rather be outside, looking in—like the little girl peering through the glass window at the intriguing rodents in a section of the zoo—or instead partake in the grand design, taking a cue from Mother Nature? If you answered yes, and if you're up for it, let's you and I follow the road on a quest to find out a particularly powerful software design approach that should not be allowed to languish anymore...

But first, FWIW, allow me to—and this is especially for those of you who are already looking for me to make things snappy—introduce three sparkling books (including the seminal one which started it all) which capture the aforementioned software design approach that we will be grappling with over the course of this essay:

1. *Implementing Domain-Driven Design* — Addison-Wesley Professional (by Vaughn Vernon)
2. *Patterns, Principles, and Practices of Domain-Driven Design* — Wrox Publishers (by Scott Millett and Nick Tune)
3. *Domain-Driven Design: Tackling Complexity in the Heart of Software* — Addison-Wesley Professional (by Eric Evans)

Each one of the books in the list above is stellar in its own right; ignore it at your own peril (just sayin'.) Curiously enough—referring here to the fine book by Vaughn Vernon—there is a lot of cowboy humor liberally sprinkled throughout the pages of his book, *Implementing Domain-Driven Design*. Overall, though, it's a book worth reading: So if riding horses isn't exactly your thing, please don't let that blemish your view of a superb book!

FWIW, I'm going to quickly add that the same author (Vaughn

Vernon) went on to write an even more awesome book called. More details—even more than you might care for!—on exactly that can be found in an essay elsewhere: *Best Reactive Programming Books*.

With that... *Whoa*, what do we have here but a cowboy—and a petrified one at that—surrounded by crisp prairie grass, looking intently at the paradoxical downtown buildings over yonder...

Something really, *really* anachronistic is going on here, methinks

4. Doing DDD—Until The Cows Come Home!

Here, then, is the real deal (cowboy humor and all) when you are ready to dive into the implementation details of Domain-Driven Design (DDD). But I hear you asking, Yo, how does this all defy dogma?

And to which I can only reply—at this time anyway—with the admonishment to please, Hold your horses! Everything comes in its own good time, and for especially those who wait!

Dogmatism aside, imagine this: Would you rather learn things through rote memorization or via discovery? Where would we be today—as a society whose fabric has been woven through vast infrastructures of inter-networking— had we settled for the de jure standard (the OSI layered model) instead of the far superior de facto standard (TCP/IP networking)?

LIVE
IMPLEMENTING
DOMAIN-DRIVEN
DESIGN
VAUGHN VERNON

5. Who Is The Best Designer Of Them All?

Wait a second, Akram, are we going hunting for mushrooms—or toadstools or whatever in the world those three bright-red spotted things growing on stalks are—just as we had settled down with a mug of coffee in hand?!

Sigh, me and my grand designs: All I was trying to do there was to bring to the forefront of your mind the organically evolving designs sprinkled by Mother Nature across the length and breadth of the natural landscapes around us...

6. Organically Evolving (Software) Designs

All the same—my grand and outlandish schemes notwithstanding—the oh-so organic evolution outgrowth of those toadstools provides us with a perfect segue into the wherewithal of DDD! And here we are going to hear from the horse's mouth (Okay, so Eric Evans is a fine human being, and an excellent one at that; I am merely using the proverbial dictum about the apocryphal horse's mouth.) Yep, Evans is the guy who started it all: DDD as we know it today was ushered into the world through his creative agency.

And you don't have to take my word for it—listen to some luminaries of our industry gushing about his work:

Yep, right there in the pic below is my copy of Evans' book, surreptitiously propped up against a hefty tome that you should *also* check out sometime, probably sooner than later, especially if you're into AI that sort of thing. It's a rather tastefully designed book: *Planning Algorithms* (Cambridge University Press) by Steven M. LaValle

LIVE
PLANNING ALGORITH

7. *Ships Laden With (Docker) Containers*

Wait a second, what in the world is that container-laden ship doing here? Docker containers anyone? Anyone?!

(Just sayin', *just* sayin' because I'd rather stay rooted in the physical realization of *building* systems versus some ivory tower stuff, and I'm not even talking about Eiffel the tower or yo, for that matter, Eiffel the *programming* language!)

But I digress.

8. The Crimson-braided Book

I love this book, tastefully crimson-braided, standing upright, bolstered at the back by the same book (Planning Algorithms from the Cambridge University Press) that we ran into earlier, of course: Patterns, Principles, and Practices of Domain-Driven Design by Scott Millett and Nick Tune is in a league of its own when it comes to imparting the wisdom in the DDD territory.

This is one of those rare, stellar software books where it's evident that great care and attention was lavished in preparing it. Profusely illustrated, clearly articulated, replete with marvelous end-of-chapter summaries, this book is a keeper. I'm a Go/Java/Scala programmer, and have been working in the Big Data area for a while, and would have preferred the code examples to be in either of these languages. But I must confess that the C# code is pristine enough in its quality that it it's easy to follow along

The content and crystal-clear presentation is abundantly evident throughout.

All-in-all, a terrific and delightful book, which is why I think of it as one of the two definitive DDD books, the other one being, of course, the seminal volume by Eric Evans himself (the classic book entitled *Domain-Driven Design: Tackling Complexity in the Heart of Software*)!

9. Representations Are Ubiquitous. And Yes, Representations Do Matter

OK, Akram, isn't it about time that you stopped rambling—we know all too well that you are a sucker for (great) books and stuff—and instead gave us the scoop on the guts of DDD for crying out loud?

So it's Akram here, saying merely this much in my defense that the deal goes like this: While DDD is not going to solve weighty issues which humanity faces—the mosaic in the picture below with love and harmony and peace suffused all over is an ideal to which we should all strive nonetheless—anytime soon, it's only fair to mention that the way it (DDD) entered my lexicon will necessarily have us take a trip back to the time. That's when I was working as a senior software engineer for Boston Scientific (not in Boston, mind you, but in the good old Twin Cities in my beloved Minnesota) and I noticed a copy of Evans' groundbreaking book sitting on the desk of one of my coworkers...

My (now-erstwhile) coworker began talking about this thing called a Ubiquitous Language and stuff like that. It made *some* sense at that time, and I actually headed over to the local Barnes & Noble that afternoon and got myself a copy of the book; the booksellers there, of course, all knew me by first name, and on seeing me enter the bookstore, realized full well that I must have found yet another excuse for buying yet another book (But they weren't complaining, at least as best as *I* could tell.)

The bottom line is this: Representation *does* matter—Would you rather work with concise JSON-encoded representations of data or with their far more verbose kin, those XML-encoded representations? Would you rather do arithmetic using the lean and efficient Arabic numerals or their laborious kin, the Roman numerals? Yep, I thought you would agree.

9. Fast-forwarding By 10 Years

That was 10 years ago. Let's fast-forward to 2018—and one more time recycling a pic that appeared above moment ago—and you have the best book published on the subject of DDD:

Patterns, Principles, and Practices of Domain-Driven Design by Scott Millett and Nick Tune can serve as a model for the best that there is in the presentation of technical material!

10. Principled Design Must Be Informed By A Ubiquitous Language

Ah yes, so I was going to give you the lowdown on the essence of DDD. It's a mindset of principled design which expects of us—the technology types—to level with the domain experts and treat them as equal partners in an approach to the design and crafting of software that is informed by a shared language (Yep, you guessed it: We're talking about the Ubiquitous Language here!)

To take the bird's eye view, we—collectively the domain experts (the SMEs) and the technology types—should remove the artificially-erected barriers in our communication and instead work hand-in-hand to accomplish more in less time.

11. Oh, The Fun We're Going To Have!

Oh my, and and I would tell you about the fun we're going to have along the way! Pure, unadulterated joy is not far off. Not far at all, in fact, provided that we jettison off the arcane approaches of yesteryear...

12. Did Someone Say… Refactor?

Wait, did somebody say something about refactoring those lumbering engines like those which appear in the pic below? Oh my, I'd rather stick to refactoring my code, with the help, of course, of DDD tactics and strategies. After all, DDD is squarely about brainstorming that's informed all the while by collaborative learning.

Actually, I'm going to take one step back—from my mention above of refactoring code—and talk some about refactoring *design* itself. I mean, are you able to sit down with paper and pencil (or stand in front of a whiteboard for that matter) and come up with a useful model right away? If you can, then you're likely in the same league as Leonardo da Vinci, and I ceremoniously —insert one drum-roll here—refer you to the following two essays:

- What is Isaacson's Leonardo da Vinci About?
- What Can Leonardo da Vinci do for Me?

Meanwhile, for us mere mortals, as we grapple with initial design models in the quest to refactor and evolve those models, it would serve us well if only we appreciated more that the model and the language (used to describe any given model) are not static entities; if not attended to properly, the the model and the language can easily devolve into a Big Ball Of Mud. Hey, nobody wants *that!*

So the lesson to draw here is: As software practitioners, not only should we tend to mercilessly refactoring our code, we should pay at least as much attention—if not more— to refactoring our software design.

13. Then There Was The Repository

Speaking of DDD tactics and strategies, allow me to introduce another DDD concept—a centrally important one at that—which deals with the notion of a Repository. See those steely-faced gents carved into Mount Rushmore as in the picture below? There you go. And look, I'm not trying to be cute here: Evan's himself—in the picture which adorns the beginning of the central chapter dealing with Repositories—presents the image of a steely faced librarian zealously guarding a bookshelf worth of books.

To cut a long story short—woohoo, no digressions for a change —pay special attention to the crucial role that repositories play in the practice of DDD.

14. I Want To Fly Like An Eagle (Or, Failing That, Like A Seagull)

Once you got that down—plus a few salient concepts such as Bounded Context, Domain Event, and Aggregate— you will surely feel the unbearable lightness of unencumbered, yet disciplined, design. Indeed, you are bound to identify with the seagull soaring above the ocean waves as in the picture below...

—Reader: Wait a sec! Are we talking seagulls or eagles or what? Can we at least get that right please?

—Akram: Sheesh, some people can be, like, *so* picky! No matter what, remember, though that

All good? Ready to proceed and meet even *more* interesting characters in our meandering DDD journey?

15. Of Meandering Neanderthals

Hoh, hoh, hoh, did somebody just say something about "...meandering journeys"? Okay, this is a bit too much to resist, and I simply can't bring myself to close out this essay without sharing some wisdom—something that could demonstrably have been garnered only by someone deep into the cavernous and meandering landscape of distributed software systems design—which is, oddly enough, by way of a riddle that spontaneously arose in my mind during the past 24 hours.

It goes like this:

Question: What do you call a Neanderthal who is prone to meandering?

Answer: A Meanderthal, but of course!

So there. Now you tell me if the connection (Nexus?) of this parable-laden wisdom to the meandering landscape of distributed software systems design isn't as clear as the day? Yes, *yes?!*

Whoa, is that a Meanderthal—tastefully attired in that oh-so demure costume or something—in the pic below or what? I mean, wow, for one thing, it's sure got a bevy of enthralled kids for its audience!

16. Lightsaber-wielding Goslings Sure Can Derail The Practice Of DDD

But no sooner had we soothed our nerves than we took a few steps in the star-board direction and came across a fierce creature as in the picture below! Exactly, didn't I tell you? Here be monsters!! All that this gosling—and no, it's not related in any way to mild-mannered James Gosling, the original and primary designer of the Java programming language—is missing is a Jedi lightsaber, and we are out of here, like, pronto!

Look, here's the deal: To practice DDD with any level of focus, we need uninterrupted quanta of concentration. We'd rather not be dealing with Jedi lightsaber-wielding goslings if we are to get anywhere with designing software that is going to power the new era that is dawning...

17. Our Ships Sail Into The Harbor

Finally, we witness how the ships have sailed onto the shore, or at least some boats have! See those trawlers and fishermen hauling in their nets after a hard day's work of the disciplined practice of DDD? Yep, it's Entities and Aggregates all the way down...

Dare I say that our friends the turtles may wish to have a word or two with us in this regard...

18. Bright, Colorful Designs

Last, but certainly not least, you may find yourself perking up at the site of the motley crew, ragtag band of mail-boxes lining a lazy street...

Honestly, answer me this: If people would only get a little creative in choosing colors for their mailboxes, wouldn't *life* itself become all that more colorful?

19. Let's Not Forget About CQRS!

As we wind down this essay, it behooves us to remain mindful of yet another player in the DDD solution space: CQRS (Command Query Responsibility Segregation). I strongly encourage you to check out the marvelous narrative on CQRS—truly one of the standout sections—in the remarkable book named *Patterns, Principles, and Practices of Domain-Driven Design* (Wrox Publishers, by Scott Millett and Nick Tune.)

In particular, they introduce the reader to the notion of CQRS without any fuss by elegantly clarifying what CQRS is in the first place!

If you are anything at all like me, you're probably eager to fire up your favorite IDE—doesn't matter which though for me it would be IntelliJ IDEA—and bang out some code to put this CQRS thingamajig into action! YMMV, but when we all succeed, all of us here in programming digressions, we may well have on our hands something like this densely packed scenario such as the one in the picture below.

I mean, where do I even begin with the richness of it all: The legion of IoT sensors in that demure house ceaselessly emitting signals, the embedded micro-controllers attached to the handful of eucalyptus trees standing tall nearby (and ready to transmit perhaps their eucalyptus oil-levels in real-time), or perhaps that sharp S-shaped band in the adjacent road where we be driving our Ferraris (feeling safe in the knowledge that intelligent road-signs will communicate to approaching vehicles and alert them to programmatically reduce their speed)?

(Akram, stop being lazy and just find and insert right here a link to the published conference paper or two that were based on your MS dissertation related to autonomously-intelligent vehicles using AI algorithms, including the trusty back-prop!)

20. Aspiring To Sublime Designs

Hey, no Ferraris for us now; not right away, anyway. Meanwhile, let's take in the penultimate picture or two below, that of the feathers of peacock.

Are you, like me, also thinking to the timeless and inimitably graceful design that is the handiwork of Mother Nature? We—all of us technology types—can only aspire to design software that is a fraction as tasteful and graceful: Truly, the journey itself is the destination.

21. Raise Your Hand If You're Still Awake…

One If By Land, Two If By Sea.
~ Henry W. Longfellow (his eponymous poem, *Paul Revere's Ride*)

Hang on, what kind of T-shirt is that, hanging on for dear life, clinging to a clothes hanger—which itself is hanging on for its life to a desultory doorknob in my sanguine study—with the lovely logo of the reactive summit which I attended in Austin not so long ago.

But here's the real deal: See that book, stoutly standing upright —Michael J. Casey's and Paul Vigna's fine book entitled *The Truth Machine: The Blockchain and the Future of Everything*—with my T-shirt in the background? And you may well be asking yourself, muttering under your breath no doubt, "Why has Akram wedged a *Blockchain* book in the guts of an essay that purportedly on *DDD?*" I wouldn't blame you one bit if you did.

Then again, I simply *have* to make sure—so I make unannounced checks using the element of surprise—that my dear readers are still awake. And I kid you not: People have been known to fall asleep smack in the middle of reading my essays, and *continue* reading while sound asleep (that being the reading analog, of course, of sleepwalking!)

In the remote case that anyone is awake and—even more remotely still—they wish to look up my write-up on Blockchain, I can gleefully point you in the direction: Blockchain Adventures!

TRUTH
MACHINE
THE BLOCKCHAIN
AND THE FUTURE
OF EVERYTHING

22. It's Now Or Never

After all has been said and done—here we tacitly acknowledge that a whole lot more has been said than done—we've reached the horizon of our journey: We are standing in front of a bridge in the countryside, a bridge that beckons us to venture outside our comfort zone. Tree-lined or not, easy or hard, straight or crooked, we simply have to cross that bridge.

Recall the image of the Tower of Babel which appears to atop this essay: Yes, far too much time has passed, far too many disconnects have taken place in the industry—technologists speaking one language and our counterparts the domain experts speaking another—that we can *no* longer afford to wring our hands in despair as we ruefully size up the situation in realizing that a lot of water has flowed under the bridge...

It's still not too late. But it is imperative that we cross the chasm. To put it in starker terms, it's now or never.

◆ ◆ ◆

A FEW MORE TESTIMONIALS

- Just in case you wanted to get to know me better still...

Neda Hantehzadeh, PhD
Senior R&D Manager
March 7, 2019, Neda worked with Akram in different groups

I collaborated with Akram at CCC as a cross-functional team member. He is one of the most intelligent and collaborative persons I ever worked with. Akram made major contributions to designing, developing, and operationalizing our hyperscale platform (Nitro), leading to a real-time application deployed to the cloud, which consumes and processes real-time streaming telematics data from IoT devices at scale, based on a stack that includes Apache Kafka, Storm, Zookeeper, DynamoDB, and REST web services in Java. He played a key role in successfully bringing in-house a significant codebase (from a startup acquisition), helped transition incoming developers into the corporation, and migrated the codebase (from an Eclipse-OSGi bundles-based build) to a standardized Maven build. The application continues to serve one of the largest insurance companies in the world. Also as part of the Architecture team, Aram performed POCs on a routine basis to assess the viability (and feasibility) of incorporating emerging tools and technologies into the corporate stack. data models, while remaining agnostic to underlying database technologies. He led the education of the sprawling Chicago-based Development teams (as part of the Learning Academy seminars) to present and roll-out the Java application framework paradigm (The effort involved travel to the Chicago HQ). In addition Akram was always actively involved in interviewing candidates to bring new talent on-board and help grow various teams (both in Architecture and in Development). As a deep learning researcher I have been so impressed by Akram's interest in AI/deep learning. He continuously kept up with deep learning and wrote his own blogs. Moreover, he even contributed to Go programming working closely with the main developers.
At his new role at Dell he now focuses on building micro-services in the service of "a vendor-neutral open source project building a common open framework for IoT edge computing".
See less

Brendan Berry
CTO AnyConnected, Inc.
August 9, 2018, Akram worked with Brendan in the same group

In my time as a developer I have noticed that there are a few people here and there who are possessed of noticeable skills or traits; these are the people you remember years later, and can point to and say "I expanded my capabilities as a result of working with that person." These are always high performers, usually exceptionally sharp, and sometimes even nice folks. Akram easily fits all of those descriptions.

I have known few other people with such a passion for learning; and, more importantly, for sharing. His unbounded enthusiasm for both the abstract and practical concepts of technology is awesome (and a little infectious, too). He simply loves to learn, to communicate, and to Do Neat Things. He seems capable of slogging through the deepest drudgery, the long hours, and the silly office politics just for the chance to apply his vast knowledge. And he's humble to a fault!

I've known far too many developers and architects who place prestige above all else; a lot of folks practice knowledge-hoarding and avoid risk-taking. Akram is practiced at balancing risk, willing to help his fellow developers even if it means putting his own work on the back burner. As for knowledge, his drive to find and to assimilate information is just staggering, and he absolutely loves to share -- and he manages to do it in a patient, accessible manner. I've personally seen him work with some "tough customers" and he has never lost his cool or his way.

I can confidently recommend him as a superb mentor, driven worker, and all-around gentle soul. See less

Shak Kathirvel
Senior Cloud Architect (Apps and Platforms) at AWS
May 30, 2018, Shak worked with Akram in different groups

In the technology profession, it is very rare and perhaps lucky to meet and work with someone who has the great personal attributes that Akram has. He is a first-rate conceptual thinker, a talented programmer, and an extraordinarily gifted writer. Add to that set of attributes the qualities of humbleness, modesty, being affable and always smiling: Akram fits the bill. I am very fortunate to know and work with him on various occasions during several projects. He is committed, dedicated, and fully involved in all the assignments he is part of. Akram is a good listener and always respects other's ideas and approaches. Being a considerate pragmatist he puts the team's interests first before his own. He accepts, agrees and cooperates with the team's consensus, approach, and collaborative solution to projects after addressing any reservations he might have had initially. Akram is proficient in building solutions with several programming toolsets and frameworks. He chooses the right toolset for a given business problem, balancing various concerns that have to be addressed for the given business requirements. Being a detailed and conceptual thinker, his approach to solutions has invariably been comprehensive and well-thought-out. Being an undeniably gifted writer, Akram's technical blogging skills are legendary. His lucid writing skills, especially when tackling highly complicated subjects, are deeply respected by his readers: Myself being one among of them! Being a talented programmer, he has made major contributions to several high-profile projects, all the way from inception to the production phase. Among other roles that he has played, Akram was a key and founding member of the team which designed and implemented the company's flagship hyper-scale platform. We are talking here about a real-time IoT streaming analytics platform that was built from the ground up in the AWS cloud infrastructure using robust and open source frameworks such as Apache Kafka, Apache Storm, plus AWS Dynamo DB in the midst of the technology stack. He also played a key role in integrating the application solution stack from a leading, innovative startup company which was acquired by CCC Information Services. In sum, Akram is a multi-faceted individual and professional and would be a valuable asset to any organization.
See less

AFTERWORD

Writing a book is a horrible, exhausting struggle, like a long bout of some painful illness. One would never undertake such a thing if one were not driven on by some demon whom one can neither resist nor understand. For all one knows that demon is simply the same instinct that makes a baby squall for attention. And yet it is also true that one can write nothing readable unless one constantly struggles to efface one's own personality. Good prose is like a windowpane
~ George Orwell, in "Why I Write" (England Your England and Other Essays)

We have come to an end, dear Reader: Not *the* end, but *an* end. The way I see it, the journey has but begun.

Along the journey, you may well have wondered, "*Man, all those pictures...*". So yeah, there's a whole another story in there. (A story for another time, to be sure.)

Meanwhile, I thank you for sharing your precious time, for spending it lingering over these pages. I can only hope that you got (substantial) value out of it...

Be sure to come back and share your reactions.

Be in touch. My coordinates, once again, are as follows. Much as I said earlier, I invite contact—via any and *all* of these:

- Blog → Programming Digressions: Essays
- LinkedIn → This is a good way to stay in touch with me
- Twitter → I occasionally do tweet
- Github: My open source contributions
- Email → It's there, *should* you wish...

ABOUT THE AUTHOR

Akram Ahmad

Blog → Programming Digressions: Essays
LinkedIn → This is a good way to stay in touch with me Twitter → I occasionally do tweet
Github → My open source contributions

www.ingramcontent.com/pod-product-compliance
Lightning Source LLC
Chambersburg PA
CBHW071238050326
40690CB00011B/2176
* 9 7 9 8 7 1 1 8 3 3 3 2 1 *